EXPERT BIDDING

AT CONTRACT BRIDGE

EXPERT BIDDING

at Contract Bridge

by

SAMUEL M. STAYMAN

with an introduction by
ELY CULBERTSON

FABER AND FABER
24 Russell Square
London

First published in mcmlii
by Faber and Faber Limited
24 Russell Square London W.C.1
Printed in Great Britain by
Latimer Trend & Co Ltd Plymouth
All rights reserved

Contents

5

Introduction

A good bridge analyst has to be a good practical player. A good bridge player, however, need not know anything about the theory of the game, and often does not. In some cases, truly great players have been totally ignorant of bridge theory, and in many cases they are simply uninterested.

Stayman is the unusual combination of a great player and a great theorist. His record as a player speaks for itself; there is hardly anyone in any part of the world who can surpass it. His contributions to the theory of the game are important ones.

In this book he expresses his approach to several difficult bidding problems. I found the book both interesting and valuable. His advice is sound, because he is a practical player. His ideas are original; and he has that rare quality, courage. He is not afraid to go contrary to the weight of conservative opinion.

Stayman has not written the usual kind of bridge book, addressed to average players. He assumes that the reader already knows a lot about bridge, and frankly addresses himself to the expert. Nevertheless, I feel that millions of 'average' players can read this book with pleasure and profit.

ELY CULBERTSON

CHAPTER I

Problems of Bidding in No-trump

Over the course of the last ten years I have worked very hard on the problem of how to bid no-trump type hands. I think that the problem is licked at last. Whether or not that is so, the record of our team in first-class competition tends to prove that we have solved it better than any of the other leading players.

Why have we gone to all this trouble? We certainly wouldn't have bothered with it if the methods in common use had been satisfactory. But they were very unsatisfactory, and we were practically compelled to search for something better.

It might take you about an hour to learn my method, and you might have to practice it two or three times before you felt quite at home with it. If you're a reasonable person, you won't go to that trouble unless you are convinced that your present method is faulty and that my method eliminates those faults without introducing others.

Therefore our first step is to see what is wrong with the methods that most bridge players—including the experts—use to bid no-trump type hands.

How Strong is the No-trump?

All the best American players agree than an opening

bid of one no-trump should be made only on a fairly strong hand. You cannot bid accurately, however, if you let it go at that. You must know the *exact* strength of the no-trump hand, and the possible strength of that hand must lie within a very narrow range.

We'll go into the reasons for that statement in a moment, but first we must make a bow to the various point-count methods of evaluating no-trump hands. There are several different point counts in general use. They are useful only if they are accurate and simple. We'll have more to say about that later on, but at this time we can make the general statement that a good point count is one step (of the many steps that are needed) in the right direction.

Let's suppose for the moment that you and your partner don't have any exact agreement on the strength needed for an opening bid of one no-trump. Your partner may bid one no-trump with any of the following three hands:

1.	2.	3.
♠ A x x	♠ A x x	♠ A Q x
♥ A J x	♥ A Q x	♥ Q J x
♦ K x x x	♦ A x x x	♦ A K x x
♣ K Q x	♣ K Q x	♣ K Q x

What are you supposed to bid, as his partner, with such a hand as:

4.   ♠ K x x   ♥ 10 x x x   ♦ Q x x   ♣ J x x

How many tricks will your partner make with such a dummy? There's no certainty, because much depends on the defence and on the length of the suit that the defenders plug away at. However, we can make a fair estimate.

With the first hand he will tend to make six or seven tricks: two in spades and four or five elsewhere.

With the second hand he will tend to make seven or eight tricks: two in each black suit and three or four in the red suits.

With the third hand he will tend to make nine or ten tricks: five in the black suits, three or four diamonds, and perhaps a heart.

Your correct course is to pass if your partner has the first or second hand. You must raise to two no-trump, however, if he has the third hand.

How do you know which type of hand your partner has? You don't; you must guess. Sometimes you will guess right. The bad guesses are usually called bad luck.

Perhaps my examples are a bit extreme. Perhaps you and your partner don't have quite such a big range for the opening bid of one no-trump. But do you know *exactly* what that range is?

Take another responding hand. You hold:

5. ♠ K x x x ♥ K x x ♦ Q J x ♣ A x x

There's no question about game, of course. The only question is whether or not to reach a slam.

If your partner has the weakest of those three sample hands, he has nine cold tricks. He would have to be unlucky to be set at four no-trump—but it *could* happen. He would need good luck to make five no-trump. There is no play at all for six no-trump.

If your partner has the middle type of hand, he will tend to make ten or eleven tricks. There is no play at all for six no-trump.

If your partner has the really strong hand, he will make six no-trump very easily.

Your correct course is to bid three no-trump if your partner has the first type of hand. Even a mild slam invitation is unsafe.

You must also bid only three no-trump if your partner has the second type of hand. If you invite the slam, your partner is bound to accept—and then the fat is in the fire.

However, you *must* invite the slam if your partner has the third type of hand. You don't want to miss a slam that's cold without even a finesse.

Lest you think that I have exaggerated the doubt and the guessing that goes on, I will show a hand that was bid and played in the expert game at the Cavendish Club in New York. The players who sat East and West have played as partners in dozens of pair contests and team matches. Each is among the first ten Life Masters. Every tournament player in the country would know their names.

Here is how they came to grief:

	West	East	West	East
6.	♠ K Q J x x	♠ A x x	Pass	1 ♥
	♥ 10 x	♥ A K J x	1 ♠	2 N-T
	♦ K x x	♦ Q 10 9 x	4 N-T	5 N-T
	♣ J x x	♣ A Q	Pass	

East didn't make five no-trump, but he had the consolation of coming close. Maybe if he played this type of hand ten times he'd make five no-trump seven or eight times. But it would be a horrible contract every single time.

Was West the culprit for bidding four no-trump? West knew that a bid of three no-trump would not show the full strength of his hand. He didn't know the exact strength of his partner's hand, and hoped that East had enough to bid and make a slam.

Was East the culprit for bidding five no-trump? He thought that he held well above minimum for his jump to two no-trump. He might have made the same bid with either of these hands:

7. ♠ A 10 x   ♥ A Q J x   ♦ J 10 9 x   ♣ A Q
8. ♠ x x   ♥ A K Q x   ♦ A J 10 x   ♣ K Q x

Since he actually held a better hand than either, he felt entitled to go on to five no-trump. He knew that West had passed originally and had bid only one spade over one heart—but there was still the possibility that West had enough material for a slam.

East's jump to two no-trump was, of course, one of the no-trump bids covered by my method. There should have been no problem at all, as we will see later on. But the hand led two of our top experts astray. What's more, you might try giving either hand to your expert friends to see whether or not *they* stay out of trouble.

It would be easy to give additional examples, but this is hardly necessary. Every experienced player is familiar with the problem. The important thing is that the problem exists and that it is a serious hazard when ordinary bidding methods are used.

There is no such problem when my bidding method is used.

The Question of Safety

When your partner opens the bidding with one no-trump and you respond with two of a suit, you expect him to bid again (if you play any of the standard systems). In some systems you can expect him to rebid only if your response is two of a major suit; but he is allowed to pass two clubs or two diamonds. In practice, even a response of two clubs or two diamonds is very seldom passed.

The reason is quite simple. The responder may wonder whether the hand should play at game in a suit or at game in no-trump. If he simply raises no-trump and never bids a suit, the hand will surely be played in no-trump. If he mentions a suit, on the way up, there is some possibility that a choice will be exercised.

This is all right when the responding hand contains a little stuff. He's quite willing to reach a game contract, and so he's perfectly satisfied to have the opening bidder rebid.

It's also all right when the responding hand is worthless except for a fairly long suit. Then he can bid two of his suit as a first response and three of his suit as a sign-off. For example, you would bid two spades and then three spades with such a hand as:

9. ♠ Q J x x x x ♥ x ♦ x x ♣ x x x x

But what do you do if you have something like:

10. ♠ Q x x x x ♥ x ♦ x x x ♣ x x x x

You're not eager to wind up at *three* spades. The opponents might wake up in time to double. If the spades are banked against you, somebody may double three spades—and then it will be costly.

Since you don't dare risk getting to three spades, you must pass one no-trump. That's almost sure to be a poor contract.

If you had your way, you would bid two spades with this hand—provided that you could shut your partner up. However, you'd have to take the muzzle off his mouth the next time you responded with two spades, for then you might have a fairly decent hand.

My bidding method solves this problem. You can't get into trouble with these miserable responding hands, and you don't risk missing a game when you have a little strength.

The 4-4 Major Suit

Nobody has much trouble with a good five-card major suit opposite an opening bid of one no-trump. You simply bid your long suit. If it's good enough, you can bid it more than once.

Practically everybody has trouble with a *four*-card major suit opposite an opening bid of one no-trump. If you never mention the suit, you may discover that you have missed the best spot. If you do mention the suit, you can't tell whether or not your partner is counting on you to have a five-card suit. And if you should happen to have *two* four-card major suits, you really have a field day showing your hand without misleading your partner.

Most good players simply give up when faced by this problem. They bid no-trump and hope for the best. After all, sometimes the opening bidder doesn't have a four-card fit; and sometimes the play for game is just about as good in no-trump as in the suit.

But then again, as every experienced player knows, the play for game in the 4-4 major may be the best. It may even be the *only* sound play for game. *This* is certainly true: if you and your partner could see each other's cards, you'd want to play the hand in the 44-major suit rather than in no-trump.

One example will probably suffice. This hand was

dealt in the 1950 Summer Championships at Columbus, Ohio.

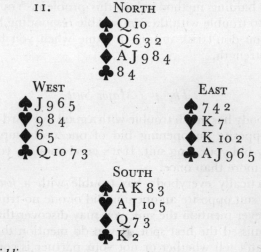

11.
NORTH
♠ Q 10
♥ Q 6 3 2
♦ A J 9 8 4
♣ 8 4

WEST
♠ J 9 6 5
♥ 9 8 4
♦ 6 5
♣ Q 10 7 3

EAST
♠ 7 4 2
♥ K 7
♦ K 10 2
♣ A J 9 6 5

SOUTH
♠ A K 8 3
♥ A J 10 5
♦ Q 7 3
♣ K 2

The bidding:

SOUTH	WEST	NORTH	EAST
1 N-T	Pass	3 N-T	Pass
Pass	Pass		

At nearly every table the bidding was substantially the same, and the final contract was three no-trump. This is a horrible contract at either rubber bridge or match-point bridge.

A club is opened, and South is allowed to make his king. He must now win eight more tricks on the run. In the actual tournament, the heart finesse succeeded, and South could take his tricks and shut up shop.

However, everybody who played the hand at three no-trump knew that he was in the wrong contract. With the heart finesse succeeding, five hearts could be made —for a far better score than three no-trump. And if

South tries to improve his score by playing the hand wide open, the loss of the diamond finesse may well cost him the contract.

At rubber bridge the average declarer would take the heart finesse, run his nine tricks, and forget about the hand. Few players are thoughtful enough to realize that three no-trump is a bad contract even if it is fulfilled.

Three no-trump stands or falls on the heart finesse. Four hearts usually makes even if both red kings and the club ace are offside.

Obviously, if you make it a practice to play hands of this kind at three no-trump you will often be set. If you play them at four of the fitting major, you will be set far less frequently.

How can this type of hand be bid properly by the methods commonly used? North surely cannot bid the ragged hearts. Should South bid spades and then hearts instead of beginning with one no-trump? That's fine if he strikes a four-card fit; otherwise there will be confusion. North may feel compelled to raise with three-card support on the assumption that South has a real two-suiter. And if North does raise, South then has to wonder whether it is a four-card or a three-card raise.

There is no such guesswork when my method is used. Incidentally, it was used with this very hand, and the proper contract of four hearts was reached absolutely automatically. We will come back to this hand in a later chapter.

Let's take a related problem. Your partner opens with *two* no-trump, and you hold:

12. ♠ J 10 x x   ♥ J x x x   ♦ K x x   ♣ x x

Obviously, you want to be in a game contract; slam

is out of the question. Just as obviously, you prefer four of a major if your partner has a four-card major suit. Otherwise three no-trump will be quite satisfactory.

How do you find out about a possible major-suit fit? In the ordinary bidding methods there is no way. You must bid three no-trump and take your chances.

Of course, your partner may happen to hold:

13. ♠ A Q x x   ♥ A Q x   ♦ A Q J x   ♣ K x

With a club opening, the contract of three no-trump will depend solely on the spade finesse. Four spades can be made even if all the missing high cards are off-side.

My bidding method gets you to the fitting major automatically. If there is no fitting major, you play the hand at three no-trump.

The Problem of Two No-trump

Your partner opens the bidding with two no-trump. You have a balanced hand that includes a king—or perhaps your only honour cards are a queen and a jack. Should you raise to three no-trump?

You want to be in three no-trump if your partner has an absolute maximum for his bid of two no-trump. Otherwise you want to leave him alone in two no-trump. For example, he may have either of the following two types of hands:

14. ♠ K Q x   ♥ K Q x   ♦ K Q x x   ♣ A K x

15. ♠ A Q x   ♥ A Q 10   ♦ A J 10 x   ♣ K Q J

Your king or queen-jack are not enough for game if he has the first hand, but they are enough to give him a reasonable play for game if he has the second hand.

Mind you, we are not now talking about hit-or-miss opening bids of two no-trump. All of the leading players in the country would bid two no-trump on either of the hands we have just supplied. That is, all the leading players except those few who use my method.

This problem does not exist in my method. As we will see, you don't raise because you know that your partner cannot possibly have that ultra-strong hand. He has another way of showing the big hand—without getting past two no-trump opposite a blank hand.

The Problem of Three No-trump

The accepted type of hand for the opening bid of three no-trump is something like this:

16. ♠ A K x   ♥ A K x   ♦ A Q 10 x   ♣ K Q J

However, some players like to make an opening bid of three no-trump with this type of hand:

17. ♠ A x   ♥ K x   ♦ A K Q x x x   ♣ J x

There is a lot to be said for each method. You've probably heard all the arguments pro and con—many times.

It would be pleasant if you could use *both* methods, depending on the nature of your hand. But then, what is your partner to do if he happens to have something like this:

18. ♠ J 10 x x x x   ♥ x x   ♦ x   ♣ x x x

Surely this hand should be played at spades if you have the powerhouse. Just as surely, your partner should pass if you have the gambling type of three no-trump bid.

This problem does not exist when you use my method. You have a way of showing each type of hand without any chance of confusing your partner. He knows when to speak up and when to keep his peace.

Is it Worth the Trouble?

I think you will agree that one or more of the problems we have discussed will plague you in any average session of bridge. The difference between guessing right and guessing wrong will probably amount to 600 points (game, tricks, and the penalty for going down). Half the time you'll guess right. So you'll lose your 600 points every other session—or about 300 points per session.

Do you care about 300 points per session? Of course you do. And remember that it may be a very conservative estimate. Perhaps your present bidding method costs you twice or three times that much.

To avoid that loss, go on with the next chapter.

CHAPTER II

Why a Point Count?

Like most bridge players I was brought up on quick tricks and honour tricks. From time to time I would hear of some eccentric who liked to count his hand by 'points'. Since these people were otherwise quite harmless, I paid no attention to them for many years.

My conversion was no sudden event. I did not wake up one morning and say penitently: 'I have walked in darkness for lo these many years, but now I have seen the light.'

I began to count my hand in points just to show how ridiculous the point count was compared to the judgment of an experienced player. Much to my surprise, it wasn't ridiculous. After a while I stopped looking for the joke that wasn't there, and I began a search for an ideal point count. In a way, this book is the result of that search.

Hundreds, perhaps thousands, of tournament players have likewise made their switch from honour tricks to point count. Some of them are generally conceded to be players of the first rank, and the rest of them range through all the other ranks.

Why does anybody switch from a familiar method to something new and different? What is the difference between honour tricks and point count?

The biggest single difference is that a high card always counts the same number of *points* but doesn't always count the same number of *honour tricks*.

Consider the following partnership hands:

	19.				20.	
WEST		EAST		WEST		EAST
♠ x x x		♠ A K x		♠ K x x		♠ A x x
♥ x x x		♥ K Q x		♥ Q x x		♥ K x x
♦ x x x		♦ A K x		♦ K x x		♦ A x x
♣ x x x x		♣ K Q x x		♣ Q x x x		♣ K x x x

The high cards in the first hand are identical with the high cards in the second hand. The point count of the partnership is the same in both hands. The count of honour tricks is not the same. The first hand counts to 6 honour tricks; the second to only $4\frac{1}{2}$ honour tricks.

Why is there a difference? You get more honour tricks for a high card if it is accompanied by a higher card in the same suit. You have combinations of that kind in the first hand, but they are broken up in the second hand.

Is this difference proper and accurate? Does it reflect a difference in the playing value of the hand?

There is no single, simple answer to these questions. The general answer is that honour tricks are more accurate than points when the opponents have most of the high cards;[1] but less accurate when *your* side has most of the high cards.

Let's take a simple example. Are the ace-king of

[1] As a matter of fact, that is how honour tricks developed. The original *quick tricks*, invented by Wilbur C. Whitehead, were based on the *defensive value* of the hand. Ely Culbertson made some changes in the quick-trick table and gave it a new name: *honour tricks*. The table of honour tricks has been changed several times since its first appearance almost twenty years ago, but it has always been based on the *defensive* value of the hand.

spades worth more than the ace of spades and the king of hearts? They count more in honour tricks, but the same in any point count.

If your partner has only low spades and hearts, the ace-king of spades are worth more. But there's no difference if your partner has high cards in those two suits, especially if he has the king of spades backing up your ace and the ace of hearts backing up your king.

This principle applies to other cases. Combinations of high cards are worth more than isolated high cards. But an isolated high spade in one hand forms a combination with an isolated high spade in the partner's hand. That sort of combination gets lost in the honour trick count; it doesn't get lost in the point count.

Is this just a theoretical argument, or is there a *practical* difference? How does it affect the bidding?

It has no effect when the partnership hands are weak. Honour tricks are more accurate in this case, but a poor hand doesn't look any better no matter how you count it. A pass is still a pass.

Let's go to the other extreme. What happens when the partnership hands are very strong? How do the two methods compare on slam bidding?

To begin with, *anybody* can bid a lay-down slam. The real art is to bid the slams that you can make and to stay out of the slams that you can't make. If your method keeps you out of too many makable slams or puts yóu into too many unmakable slams, it is an inaccurate method.

How do you know in advance whether a slam is makable or unmakable? The simplest way is to know definitely how much high-card strength your side has and how much the other side has. You can afford to bid a small slam in no-trump if the opponents hold somewhat less than an ace and a king, and your method should tell you whether or not they do.

Here are a couple of hands to test on this basis:

	21.			22.	
WEST		EAST	WEST		EAST
♠ A Q 10		♠ K x x	♠ A K J		♠ Q x x
♥ A Q x		♥ K 10 x	♥ A K x		♥ Q J 10
♦ K x x		♦ A Q x	♦ Q J x		♦ A K x
♣ K x x x		♣ A Q x x	♣ 10 x x x		♣ Q J x x

In each case the partnership total is 8 honour tricks. In the first hand you have either twelve or thirteen tricks, depending on the break in clubs. In the second hand you have no play for twelve tricks. The opponents must take two high clubs.

Why should hands that have the same value in honour tricks produce such different results? Combinations have played you false. The total number of honour tricks in the pack varies according to the way the high cards are combined. Consequently, you can't always tell from your own total exactly how much is held by the other side.

What happens when you apply a point count to these two hands? You don't get the same total for the two hands. No matter which point count you use, you will find that there is an important difference between the two hands.

You are bound to discover in the first hand that the opponents may have four jacks or a couple of queens, or an ace, or something of that value—but not more. And using a *good* point count, you are bound to discover in the second hand that the opponents have something like a king and two queens, or an ace and a king, or something of that value. If you are reasonably prudent, you bid a slam in the first hand but stay out of a slam in the second hand.

Let's go down the scale a bit.

23.	24.	25.
NORTH	NORTH	NORTH
♠ K x x	♠ x x x	♠ Q J x
♥ K x x	♥ x x x	♥ Q J x
♦ A K x x	♦ x x x	♦ K Q x x
♣ x x x	♣ K x x x	♣ K x x
SOUTH	SOUTH	SOUTH
♠ A Q x	♠ A K x	♠ K x x
♥ A x x	♥ A K x	♥ K x x
♦ x x x	♦ A K x x	♦ J 10 x
♣ A K x x	♣ x x x	♣ A J 10 x

In the first hand the partnership total is 7½ honour tricks. That total may sometimes put you in the slam zone, but in this case you have nine cold tricks and no play at all for a slam. That is exactly what any good point count would tell you.

In the second hand the partnership total is 6½ honour tricks. That total should give you a very comfortable play for game, but it doesn't. You have practically no chance to make three no-trump. Once again, that is exactly what any good point count would tell you.

In the third hand the partnership total is only 5 honour tricks. That should *not* give you a good play for game. But you actually have a very fine play for three no-trump. And, once more, any good point count would tell you that you had a good chance for game.

In all three cases the count of honour tricks gives you a *false* idea of the value of the partnership cards. In all three cases the count of points gives you an *accurate* idea of the value of the partnership cards.

Mind you, no point count is 100 per cent accurate. If your partner has K-Q-x of a suit, your A-x-x is worth just as much as A-J-10. No point count will tell you that. No point count will tell you before the dummy goes down exactly how the high cards in the two hands will 'fit'. But neither, of course, will any other method of valuing a hand tell you such things.

In other words, the point count method is not perfect. It's simply the best method there is.

If you were a point counter before, or if this argument has convinced you, the next chapter will have special interest for you. If you still prefer to use honour tricks, you can skip the next chapter and go on to the one that follows it. Most of my bidding methods can be used on the basis of honour tricks. They will not be, however, as accurate as they would be if you used my point count.

CHAPTER III

The Ideal Point Count

The ideal point count must be:

1. *Accurate*. It must translate card values faithfully into point values. It must lead you automatically to the bid that would be made by the most precise expert.

2. *Simple*. It must deal in small numbers and must be easy to remember. It must be applicable, with a minimum of special rules or adjustments, to all bidding situations—whether for suit or no-trump contracts.

The late George Reith used to advocate a count of 6 for the ace, 4 for the king, 3 for the queen, 2 for the jack, and 1 for the ten.

A count of 7-5-3-2-1 for the five honour cards was once used in some countries of Europe. Both counts are pretty accurate, especially the latter. Neither, however, is simple.

The Four Aces count is 3 for the ace, 2 for the king, 1 for the queen and ½ for the jack. This is very good for suit bidding but needs adjustment for no-trump bidding.[1] I used this count for many years and consider it

---

[1] For various no-trump situations it is necessary to correct for a different number of honour cards. This system, devised by Oswald Jacoby and Howard Schenken, is very accurate, and I am happy to say that it is just about identical for no-trump bidding with the (much simpler) count that I recommend in this book.

nearly perfect in every respect but one: *simplicity*. Only a few players have taken the trouble to master this count, and I've therefore had to look around for an accurate count that the average experienced player could pick up painlessly.

The most popular count (devised by Bryant McCampbell in 1914 but known as the 'Work' count because first widely publicized by Milton C. Work) is 4 for the ace, 3 for the king, 2 for the queen, and 1 for the jack. This is simple, and has become very popular, but it isn't accurate. Fortunately, it can be transformed into an accurate method by a very simple adjustment.

The Stayman count is the same as the Work count except that you add ½ point for each ace or ten in your hand. For slam purposes you do not count the tens. In other words, the count is:

Ace	King	Queen	Jack	Ten
4½	3	2	1	½

Thousands of players use the Work count without the Stayman 'correction'. What is wrong with the original count, and how does my change improve matters?

The Work count undervalues the ace compared to the other high cards. As a result, it gives too low a value to a hand that contains aces; and too high a value to a hand that contains no aces. This false valuation sometimes makes a difference in your first bid; and, when it doesn't, it makes a difference in your impression of your rebid values.

Let's see how this works out with actual hands.

26.	Work Count	Stayman Count
♠ A 10 x	4	5
♥ A x x	4	4½
♦ A J 10	5	6
♣ Q 10 x x	2	2½
	—	—
	15	18

In the Work count, as practised by most players to-day, you need 16 points as a minimum for an opening bid of one no-trump. This hand is not good enough according to that count. In my count, you need 17½ points for an opening bid of one no-trump. This hand is better than an absolute minimum, and it's worth the bid.

Now let's take an aceless hand.

27.	Work Count	Stayman Count
♠ K Q x	5	5
♥ K Q x	5	5
♦ Q J x	3	3
♣ K 10 x x	3	3½
	—	—
	16	16½

In the Work count, this hand qualifies for an opening bid of one no-trump. In my count it doesn't.

Just compare those two hands. Forget about points and think only as a bridge player. Is hand 27 better than hand 26? It is actually worse. Any accurate method of valuation would tell you so. And any good bidding method should be based on accurate valuation.

It simply doesn't make good bridge sense to bid one

no-trump on these aceless wonders—and to say at the same time that a stronger hand doesn't qualify.

Let's see what happens to a hand with four aces.

28.		Work Count	Stayman Count
♠	A 10 x	4	5
♥	A 10 x	4	5
♦	A x x	4	4½
♣	A 10 x x	4	5
		16	19½

This hand barely qualifies for a no-trump bid in the Work count. It's only a half-point short of absolute maximum for a no-trump bid in my count. Put the fourth ten in there and it would be a maximum for me but still only a minimum in the Work count.

Again forget about point counts and think only as a bridge player. Is that a minimum no-trump bid? Is it in the same class as the aceless wonder we have just examined?

Here's a stronger aceless hand to compare with it.

29.		Work Count	Stayman Count
♠	K Q x	5	5
♥	K Q x	5	5
♦	K Q J	6	6
♣	Q x x x	2	2
		18	18

This hand is a near-maximum in the Work count. It's only a half-point better than a dead minimum in my count.

Compare it with hand 28. It's considerably stronger than the four-ace hand, says the Work count. It's considerably weaker says my count. Which hand would *you* rather hold?

'Forget about such small differences,' say some of the advocates of the Work count. 'It's inaccurate here and there, but it all comes out in the wash. By the time you've added all your points, an undervaluation here counterbalances an overvaluation there—and the result is just perfect.'

As we have seen, this just isn't so. The errors don't cancel out. And there's no need to use an inaccurate method when a very simple correction will make it accurate. Would you use a defective adding machine on the theory that the totals would be approximately correct in the long run—or would you have it repaired?

Summary of the Stayman Count

Card	Points	
Each ace	4½	If you are used to the Work
Each king	3	count, add your hand as usual.
Each queen	2	Then add ½ point for each ace and
Each jack	1	each ten.
Each ten	½	

Five-card usable suit, 1 point; six-card usable suit, 2 points.

Tens are not counted for slam purposes. (This adjustment is made only when the bidding takes a slammish turn.)

Total points
in pack   44   *Shading:* The values needed for
Game in   game or slam may be slightly shad-
  no-trump 27½   ed when there is a good suit fit. A

Small slam 35 vulnerable side may bid game with
Grand slam 39 only 27 points.

A *usable* five-card suit is one headed by two of the
four top honours. Such a suit as A-10-x-x-x, K-10-x-x-x,
or Q-10-x-x-x may be valued at ½ point for length. A
usable six-card suit is one headed by ace, king, or
queen. Weaker long suits may gain length valuation if
the bidding discloses a fit in partner's hand.

It is important to keep in mind the number of points
required for game, small slam, and grand slam. As the
bidding develops, you find out how many points your
partner holds. Add them to your own points, and you
have the partnership total. Compare that total with
the figures you have in mind, and you will know
whether you are headed for game, small slam, or grand
slam.

You will not make every game or slam that you bid
on these calculations. If you did, those would be the
wrong figures to keep in mind.

An expert wants to be in a game if he has somewhat
less than an even chance to make it (provided that there
is no risk of a penalty double). For a small slam, he is
content with a shade better than an even chance. For
a grand slam, he wants favourable odds of a bit less
than 3 to 1.[1]

[1] Mathematically, 2 to 1 odds are good enough, but most good players
rightly want more favourable odds for a grand slam. They are willing to
gamble a few hundred points at a time because they will get many game
and small-slam hands and will therefore have a fair chance to win back
on successful gambles what they lose on unsuccessful gambles. Grand
slams, however, are so rare that to gamble on a grand slam hand is like
doubling your usual stakes for one or two hands a month! Luck becomes
too important a factor to suit the taste of the player who prides himself
on his skill.

The figure of 27½ for game in no-trump will give you the right kind of percentage play. When you are vulnerable, you can afford to bid game on a skimpier chance because the value of game is greater than when you are not vulnerable, whereas the value of making only a part score remains the same whether you are vulnerable or not. Hence you can afford to shade your requirements down to 27 points when you are vulnerable.

When you bid a small slam with 35 points, the opponents have 7 points. They cannot have an ace and a king, since those would total 7½ points. Whatever else they do have, you should have an even chance for the slam.

When you bid a grand slam with 39 points, the opponents may have a king. At worst, therefore, you will have a finesse for the slam. Sometimes you will not need the finesse. Sometimes the enemy may have only a queen and a jack or three jacks instead of a king. There may be thirteen cold tricks without a finesse.

You will seldom find yourself in a game or slam with the dead minimum. In exchanging information with your partner, you will usually have to guess whether he has a half-point more or less. If you are conservative in such guesses (not a bad idea in slam bidding), you will usually wind up with an 'extra' point or so.

CHAPTER IV

The Opening Bid of One No-trump

The opening bid of one no-trump shows the nature of your distribution and the amount of your high-card strength within very narrow limits. It describes your hand so completely, and the later development of the bidding is so easy, that you should prefer to open with one no-trump whenever your hand qualifies for that bid.

Requirements

Distribution: 4-3-3-3
4-4-3-2 } no worthless
5-3-3-2 } doubleton
Strength: 17½ points to 20 points
never less   never more

Some variation may be desired when the hand contains a five-card suit. My own experience leads me to bid one no-trump anyway, whether the suit is major or minor. However, since this is a matter on which there is an arguable difference of opinion, I will give no example of opening no-trumps with a five-card major suit.

30.   ♠ A J x x   ♥ K 10 x x   ♦ A x   ♣ K J x

Do not hesitate to bid one no-trump even when you

have two four-card majors. If there is a 4-4 fit in either major, you will find out about it in good time.

31. ♠A 10 x   ♥A 10 x   ♦A 10 x   ♣Q J x x

This is a typical minimum opening bid of one no-trump. It counts only 15 points according to the Work count, and some players would therefore consider it too weak for an opening bid of one no-trump. If this hand were opened with one club, it would be difficult to find an accurate rebid. When it is opened with one no-trump, there is no rebid problem; the entire value and nature of the hand has been described in one bid.

32. ♠A J x   ♥A x x   ♦A x   ♣Q J x x x

This hand counts to 18½ points, if one point is counted for length in clubs. An opening bid of one no-trump is a far better total description of this hand than an opening bid of one club.

33. ♠K J x x   ♥K x   ♦A Q x x   ♣K Q x

18½ points with every suit well stopped. The 4-4-3-2 distribution is far more frequently held than the 4-3-3-3. A precise opening bid of one no-trump is a firm foundation for the bidding of any hand. It is therefore a mistake to limit no-trump bids to the relatively infrequent 4-3-3-3.

34. ♠K Q x   ♥A J x x   ♦K 10 x   ♣K J 10

18½ points with prospects of a double stopper in nearly every suit. This is the middle range of the opening no-trump bid.

35. ♠K x   ♥K J x   ♦K Q x x x   ♣A J x

18½ points, counting one point for length in diamonds. The doubleton suit must be at least K-x. If a hand is otherwise ideal for an opening bid of one no-trump, some experts will stretch a point and bid it with Q-x in the weak suit.

36. ♠ A J x x   ♥ K 10 x   ♦ A x   ♣ A J x x

With 19 points we enter upon the maximum range of the opening bid of one no-trump. However, the difference between this hand and hand 30 (the minimum no-trump) is only the difference between the ace and the king of clubs.

37. ♠ K J x   ♥ A x   ♦ K x x   ♣ A Q x x x

19 points, counting one point for the long clubs. The 5-3-3-2 distribution is almost half again as frequent as the 4-3-3-3. It pays to open such a hand with one no-trump if you have the necessary strength and stoppers.

38. ♠ A Q 10   ♥ K J x x   ♦ K Q x x   ♣ K 10

19½ points with all suits well stopped. This is a fine maximum no-trump.

39. ♠ A Q x   ♥ K Q x   ♦ A Q x x   ♣ J 10 x

19½ points with three suits very well stopped. It would be even better to have a stopper in the fourth suit also, but one cannot always have everything. Despite the weakness in clubs, this is a perfectly sound opening bid of one no-trump.

40. ♠ Q J x   ♥ A Q   ♦ K Q 10 x   ♣ A 10 x x

20 points with all suits well stopped. This is an absolutely maximum opening bid of one no-trump.

41. ♠ K Q x   ♥ K Q   ♦ K Q x   ♣ K Q x x x

Bid one club. This hand adds up to 21 points, counting one for the length in clubs. It is slightly too good for an opening bid of one no-trump.

42. ♠ Q J x   ♥ Q J x   ♦ K Q x   ♣ K Q J x

Bid one club. This hand counts to only 17 points, not enough for a sound opening bid of one no-trump. Note that this would be a perfectly acceptable opening bid of one no-trump if the uncorrected Work count is used.

43. ♠ K x   ♥ A x   ♦ A Q x x x   ♣ K J x x

Bid one diamond. With a distribution of 5-4-2-2 it usually pays to begin with one of the suits rather than with no-trump. You may eventually rebid in no-trump, but your opening bid should say something about one of your suits.

44. ♠ A   ♥ K Q x x   ♦ K Q x x   ♣ K Q x x

Bid one heart. An opening bid of one no-trump guarantees balanced distribution. The 4-4-4-1 distribution is not balanced. This hand may eventually be played in no-trump, but it would be unwise to make an opening bid in no-trump.

45. ♠ x x   ♥ K Q J   ♦ A J 10 x   ♣ A Q x x

Bid one diamond. The worthless doubleton in spades rules out an opening bid of one no-trump.

46. ♠ 10 x x x   ♥ 10 x x x   ♦ A K   ♣ A K Q

Bid one club. A suit containing four to the ten can be considered almost stopped. However, it does not pay to open a hand with one no-trump when the hand contains *two* such doubtful stoppers. An opening bid of one no-trump should really guarantee three suits stopped.

The strongest possible bid of one no-trump is better than the weakest possible hand by only 2½ points—the value of a queen and a ten. It may seem that this range is so narrow that all opening bids of one no-trump should be considered equal. However, this is not so.

A hand that counts 17½ to 18½ points is considered a minimum no-trump. A hand that counts 19 to 20 points is considered a maximum no-trump.

This distinction does not mean anything so far as your opening bid is concerned. You still bid one no-trump whether you have a minimum or a maximum. However, you make a mental note about whether you were minimum or maximum. In rebidding, you will often bid a maximum one way and a minimum in a different way.

There is no danger in making sharp distinctions between hands that are so very nearly equal. No matter how strong or weak a rebid you may make later on, your partner always remembers that you opened the hand with one no-trump. The total strength of your hand must therefore lie between 17½ and 20 points.

CHAPTER V

Responses to One No-trump

When your partner has opened the bidding with one no-trump you know that his count is $17\frac{1}{2}$ to 20 points. You can count your own points, add them to those shown by your partner, and compare them with the three key figures.

1. $27\frac{1}{2}$ points for game at no-trump or a major suit.
2. 35 points for a small slam.
3. 39 points for a grand slam.

There are eight different types of response that you can make. The moment you choose *one* of these eight, you indicate at the same time that your hand is not best described by any of the *other seven*. It follows that you cannot pick your best response unless you are well acquainted with all eight types.

Here they are, briefly summarized:

Response	*The Future of the Hand*
Pass	No possible game.
2♠, 2♥, or 2♦	Game unlikely at best.
2 N-T	Game probable.
3 N-T	Game, but no possible slam.
3 of any suit	Game, no slam.
Game in suit	Game, no slam.
4 or more N-T	Slam try.
2♣	The 'Stayman' Convention—subse-

> quent bidding will show whether the
> hand is headed for less than game,
> game, or slam.

Some hands call very clearly for a certain type of bid; others offer you a choice. If you have a borderline case you must look for a way to find out what you want to know without getting too high and without risking a premature pass.

You never have to consider all eight possibilities for any particular hand that you happen to hold. For example, if you're wondering about a slam, you never dream of passing as a first response. Your choices can be briefly summarized as follows:

1. *Weak Hands* (0 to 7 points): Pass or bid two of a suit.

2. *Fair Hands* ($7\frac{1}{2}$ to about $14\frac{1}{2}$ points): Raise to two or three no-trump; jump to three or more of a suit; bid two clubs.

3. *Strong Hands* (15 or more points): Jump to four or more no-trump; bid two clubs.

We will now take up each type of response in detail. As you read about each, think about how it differs from its closest neighbours. In that way, you can see how you should tend to bid a borderline hand and how your bidding changes as the hand becomes stronger or weaker or as the distribution changes slightly.

The Pass

You pass when there is no chance for game and no safe way to improve the contract. Since your hand is weak, your only question is whether, on some hands, to bid a long suit or to pass.

You have practically no choice when your distribution is 4-3-3-3, 4-4-3-2, or even 4-4-4-1. The chances are that your partner is as well off in no-trump as you would be in a suit—and he may be better off. With such flat distributions you can afford to pass with as many as 7 points. The combined total can reach only 27 points even if your partner has an absolute maximum.

When you have a five-card or longer suit, you may or may not bid. You look for the safety of a suit contract if you have a singleton or a void suit. You give your partner a chance to rebid (which he may do with a maximum count and an ideal fit) if you have very close to $7\frac{1}{2}$ points, counting your length as well as your high cards. If you have no reason to be either worried or ambitious, you simply pass.

47. ♠ x x x x x ♥ x x x ♦ x x x ♣ x x

Pass. What else can you do? There is, of course, no excuse at all for bidding a hopeless hand. You will bid your five-card suit if one no-trump is doubled; otherwise, you must sit tight and hope for the best.

48. ♠ Q x x ♥ Q x x ♦ Q x x ♣ x x x x

Pass. Even if partner has his maximum of 20 points, the combined total will be only 26—not enough for game. One or two no-trump should be made very comfortably. If an opponent doubles, you are ready to redouble; and you are willing to double any further bid.

49. ♠ K x x x x ♥ x x x ♦ x x x ♣ x x

Pass. There is no need to disturb the contract of one no-trump. Game must be out of the question, since even if partner has solidifying spades, he cannot have four fast outside winners.

50. ♠ x ♥ x x x x ♦ J x x x ♣ x x x x

Pass. You are very unhappy, but you must beware of jumping out of the frying-pan into the fire. Even if you could make a final bid at this point, you wouldn't know which suit to choose; and you certainly don't want to start a *series* of bids with this rubbish!

The Simple Take-out

In general, when your response to one no-trump is a take-out into two of a suit, you must expect your partner to pass. He is allowed to rebid only if he has a maximum no-trump (19 to 20 points) together with a magnificent fit for your suit. Experience shows that your partner must pass your response at least nine times out of ten.

Naturally, you do not want to be left in a contract of two spades or thereabouts if the combined hands can produce a game. Therefore you must never respond with two of a suit when you have a good hand. (A 'good' hand is one that contains 8 points or more; and even 7½ points may be enough for real action.)

Here we must note one exception to the rule. A response of two clubs obliges your partner to rebid. This response will be discussed shortly in great detail. At this moment, it is enough to remember that a response of two spades, two hearts, or two diamonds is not forcing and that your partner will probably pass any such response.

You should have one of two different reasons for bidding two of your suit:

1. *Fear*. Your hand is worthless at no-trump but strong enough at your suit to justify increasing the contract.

44

2. *Ambition.* Your hand is not worth a strong bid, but game is likely if your partner can rebid (with a maximum no-trump and a magnificent fit). If your partner cannot rebid, you are satisfied to play the hand at two of your suit.

Before we proceed, let us see what your partner is allowed to rebid. He will not get excited just because he has a good hand. He has already told you about it, and there is very little that he can add to his story. After all, the difference between the weakest possible and the strongest possible no-trump is less than a king.

If you respond with two spades, two hearts, or two diamonds, your partner must pass or raise your suit to three. He has no other choice. If he raises your suit to three, he guarantees a maximum no-trump together with A-K-x, A-Q-x, or K-Q-x in your suit. If your suit is a major, he is allowed to raise with any four-card fit for your suit and a maximum no-trump.

If you respond with two clubs, your partner must rebid. However, his rebid must be at the level of two. The various rebids have definite meanings, as we shall see, but all we need to know now is that your partner cannot make any rebid higher than two no-trump.

Suppose you bid two of your suit out of fright. What is the worst that your partner can do? At most he can bid three of your suit. And then you can pass. Even if you have bid two clubs, your partner cannot prevent you from bidding *three* clubs at your next turn. And then he will always pass unless he has a fine fit and a maximum no-trump. (In such cases he will bid three no-trump, and he should have an excellent play for it.)

In other words, it is safe for you to bid two of your suit when you have a very poor hand that is quite worthless at no-trump. You will probably play the hand at two of your suit; and, at worst, you can be sure of playing the hand at no higher contract than three of your suit.

If you have bid because of ambition rather than fear, you will naturally welcome a rebid by your partner. In that case, of course, you intend to take a shot at game if your partner has the material for a rebid.

51. ♠ Q x x x x ♥ x ♦ x x x ♣ x x x x

Bid two spades. This hand was mentioned in an earlier chapter. You are afraid of one no-trump and think that you will be better off at two spades. If you are obliged to play at three spades, a fit is guaranteed, and no serious damage will result.

52. ♠ x x ♥ x x x x x x ♦ x x ♣ x x x

Bid two hearts. At no-trump this hand is quite worthless. At hearts it will produce about three trump tricks at worst. Since you gain three tricks by playing the hand at hearts, you can afford to get one trick higher. If your partner can raise, your hand will be worth still more at hearts.

53. ♠ x ♥ x x x ♦ x x x ♣ Q 10 9 x x x

Bid two clubs. Your partner will rebid, and then you must proceed to three clubs. Since you commit yourself to bid to the level of three, you need a fairly decent suit. With a weak five-card suit it is wiser to let your partner struggle at one no-trump.

54. ♠ A x x x x ♥ x ♦ J x x ♣ x x x x

Bid two spades. This is not a fearful bid. You should be very comfortable at two spades if your partner passes. If he bids three spades, you may choose between a pass and a game bid. This would be a very close decision.

An extra jack would be enough to tilt the scales in favour of a game bid.

55. ♠ x   ♥ K x x x x x   ♦ x x x   ♣ Q x x

Bid two hearts. The hand counts 5 points for high cards and 2 points for length. There should be a play for game if partner has the material for a raise. If he cannot raise, two hearts should be a very comfortable contract.

56. ♠ x x   ♥ x x   ♦ Q x x x x x x   ♣ x x

Bid two diamonds. Game is possible if partner has A-K-x of diamonds. If he can raise your suit, you will take a shot at three no-trump—with seven diamond tricks as the backbone of that contract. Your action would be similar even if your suit were a major.

Borderline Cases with Weak Hands

. When you have a weak hand, your only problem is whether to pass or bid two of a suit. Your best action depends partly on your strength and partly on your distribution. The weaker your hand and the more balanced your distribution, the more you incline to a pass; the stronger your hand (up to a maximum of 7 points, of course) and the more unbalanced your distribution, the more you incline to a bid.

It's easy when you have a weak hand with balanced distribution. You must pass. It's equally easy when you have an unbalanced hand with nearly 7 points. You bid. You have a problem when you have strength without good distribution, or good distribution without strength.

57. ♠ Q x x   ♥ Q x x   ♦ Q x x   ♣ J x x x

Pass. You are tempted to bid with only 7 points because your count is made up of four honour cards. If the hand contained another ten, you would bid two clubs. If you decided to bid two clubs or even two no-trump without that other ten, you couldn't be seriously criticized. Just remember that a slight stretch by you plus a slight stretch by your partner often equals a bad set.

58. ♠ x x x x x   ♥ x x x   ♦ x   ♣ x x x x

Pass. You would surely bid two spades if one no-trump were doubled by either opponent. You can almost bid it over a pass. The suit is so weak, however, that you can't be sure you are improving the contract. You would bid the spades if they were headed by the queen or even by jack-ten; or if they were six cards in length in any case.

59. ♠ x x   ♥ x x x x x   ♦ x x x x x   ♣ x

Bid two hearts. Likewise if the distribution were 5-5-3-0. No guarantee goes with this bid. Conceivably, you may be better off at one no-trump; and you would surely be better off at one no-trump undoubled than two hearts doubled. If the diamond spots are appreciably stronger, bid two diamonds rather than two hearts.

Free Responses to One No-trump

As we have seen, the responder can show a weak hand by passing or by making a simple take-out to two spades, two hearts, or two diamonds. The meaning of such a response is not altered if the opponents enter the bidding. For example:

South	West	North	East
1 N-T	2 ♦	2 ♠	—

North's bid is not forcing and does not show a strong

hand. If he had a good hand he would double, raise in no-trump, or bid at the level of three (or higher).[1]

When the responder bids freely at the level of two, he shows a five-card or six-card suit in a hand that usually contains up to 7 points. The absolute maximum, including values for length, is $7\frac{1}{2}$ points, and this is rarely held because the responder can sometimes bid two no-trump or three of his suit with $7\frac{1}{2}$ points (and will surely do so with a better hand). The minimum would be about $4\frac{1}{2}$ or 5 points, because there is no need to get into the auction with a weaker hand; the opener does not need to be rescued, and there is no virtue in meeting trouble three-quarters of the way.

In short, the responder bids almost exactly as though there had been no intervening bid. If he had intended to bid two of his suit, he can do so (provided his suit is higher than the opponent's). If he had intended to bid two no-trump (or a choice between a conventional two clubs and two no-trump) he can bid two no-trump.

The opener may rebid with a maximum no-trump and a fine fit for responder's suit; but otherwise passes. If responder has raised to two no-trump, opener will pass with a minimum no-trump. With a maximum no-trump, he will go on—but not to three no-trump unless he has a sound holding in the opponent's suit. Opener can usually find some sort of waiting bid—even if he has to bid the opponent's suit. This will give responder a chance to show a five-card major suit, if he has one; or to raise opener's waiting bid, if the opener has shown a four-card major.

It must be admitted that the development of the bidding is more difficult when an opponent steps into the auction. Real chaos would result if responder failed

[1] A free response at the level of three (or higher) is forcing to game.

to take action with hands of the nature just described. If he passed, the opener might feel compelled to take some action; and then responder wouldn't know whether the opener had a minimum or a maximum. The partnership would proceed by guesswork and would get unnecessarily bad results.

The bidding has proceeded:

SOUTH	WEST	NORTH	EAST
1 N-T	2 ♦	?	—

60. ♠ Q J x x x   ♥ x x x   ♦ x   ♣ J x x x

Bid two spades. This is about the weakest hand that qualifies for a free bid. The count is 4 for high cards and 1 for length in spades.

61. ♠ K J 9 x x   ♥ Q 10 x x   ♦ x   ♣ x x x

Bid three spades. The count is only $7\frac{1}{2}$ points, including 1 point for length in spades. If there had been no intervening bid, the response would be two clubs (conventional), and the hand might be played for less than game. This is no longer possible, and responder must choose between the slight stretch to three spades and the decided underbid of two spades.

62. ♠ Q J x x x   ♥ K x x   ♦ x x   ♣ J x x

Bid two no-trump. With a count of 8 points, responder must make an encouraging bid. The spades are too weak for a jump, so he must bid two no-trump. This response shows general values of 8 to 9 points but does not guarantee a stopper. If the opener has a maximum no-trump, he will go on; but he can make a waiting bid, and responder will then show his spades.

63. ♠ Q J x x x   ♥ K x x   ♦ J x x   ♣ x x

Double or bid two no-trump, depending on vulnerability. This is practically the same as the last hand, except that you now have prospects of a trump trick against the opponents. You should surely double if not vulnerable against vulnerable opponents; and should surely bid two no-trump if vulnerable against non-vulnerable opponents. If vulnerability is even, the best course depends somewhat on the bidding habits of the overcaller. You tend to double a player who makes bad overcalls, but tend to bid two no-trump behind a very conservative player. Exchange the hearts and diamonds, and you tend to double any player with even vulnerability. If you had a fourth diamond, you would double regardless of vulnerability.

Strong Responses to One No-trump

Logically enough, any response other than a pass or a simple take-out is either mildly or strongly encouraging. When the responder has the values for an encouraging response, he tends to bid two clubs more often than anything else.

To be more specific, the best response may be two clubs on hands where the 'natural' bid may be two no-trump, three no-trump, three of a suit, or some immediate slam try. Hence any full discussion of these natural bids must always lead to a discussion of the two-club response. We will therefore proceed to a full explanation of the two-club response (usually called the 'Stayman' Convention) before we can take up the other encouraging responses.

First, however, we can summarize the meaning of those other encouraging responses:

Raise to 2 N-T: 8½ to 9 points.

Raise to 3 N-T: 9½ to 14½ points. Opener must pass.

Three of a Suit: A good suit (five or six cards) with a minimum of 9½ points. Maximum, to be discussed more fully later, is about 12 points (including points for length).

Immediate Slam Try: 15 points or more.

We will return to all of these bids, but let us first examine the response of two clubs.

CHAPTER VI

The 'Stayman' Convention

The bidding method that has become known as the 'Stayman' Convention was not named by me. I was the first to describe it in print (in the *Bridge World* in 1945), and bridge players who discussed it called it by my name.

A fairer name would be the Rapée-Stayman Convention. I say this because it began as an original idea of my friend and most regular partner, George Rapée; and was developed in our partnership.

We had been working on the problem of getting to a good major suit contract after an opening bid of one no-trump, and we had tried one or two ideas that turned out to be unsatisfactory. One day George suggested that the responder bid two clubs (artificially) to invite the opening bidder to show whether or not he had a four-card major; and, in the absence of a major, to show whether he held a maximum or a minimum no-trump.

The latter feature has been at least as valuable as finding the suit fit. Moreover, this feature serves to distinguish the convention from various other artificial responses of two clubs.

During the last six years George Rapée and I have used the convention and have extended its application to other no-trump situations. We have developed it from a general idea to a very delicate and precise tool. Moreover, we have worked out patterns of subsequent bids, each with its own distinct meaning, in order to lead the partnership as often as possible to the best contract.

The fundamental idea of the convention is fairly well known among the tournament players of the United States. Many of those players use it in a garbled form, perhaps because a really full explanation of the bid has never before been available. It is possible that some players will prefer to stick to their own version even after they have become acquainted with the genuine article. If so, my feelings will not be hurt; I wish them good luck.

Anybody has the right to use a two-club convention. But we have experimented with ever so many variations, and we think that our present method is the best.

The Fundamental Idea

Your partner opens the bidding with one no-trump, and you respond by bidding two clubs. The opener has no idea of the nature of your hand. You may have a hand of almost any strength and of almost any distribution. If you really have a club suit, that would be sheer coincidence. This doesn't matter, because the opener is not allowed to pass at this moment.[1]

At his next turn the opener must show a major suit if he has one. Lacking a biddable major suit (Q-x-x-x or better), he must indicate whether he has a maximum or a minimum no-trump.

[1] Exception: With a part score of 60 or more, a response of two clubs is natural, not conventional.

When he has told his story, the next move will be up to you. Before we proceed with that next move, let us see how the opener rebids over two clubs.

The bidding has proceeded:

OPENER	RESPONDER
1 N-T	2 ♣
?	

If the opener has biddable spades (Q-x-x-x or better), he bids two spades. If he has biddable hearts, he bids two hearts. If he has biddable holdings in both majors he bids two spades and waits for a chance to show the hearts later.

If the opener has no biddable major suit, he must show the *size* of his no-trump. The range of possible no-trumps is from $17\frac{1}{2}$ to 20 points. The lower half, $17\frac{1}{2}$ to $18\frac{1}{2}$, is the range of minimum no-trumps. The upper half, 19 to 20 points, is the range of maximum no-trumps. With a minimum no-trump and no biddable major suit, the opener's rebid is two diamonds; with a maximum no-trump and no biddable major suit, the opener's rebid is two no-trump.

The Opener's First Rebid

The bidding has proceeded:

OPENER	RESPONDER
1 N-T	2 ♣
?	

64. ♠ Q x x x   ♥ A Q J   ♦ K 10 x   ♣ K J 10

Bid two spades. You have a minimum no-trump and a minimum biddable suit, but it makes no difference. Yours not to reason why—at this stage, anyway. You have been asked to show a biddable major suit, and you do so.

65. ♠ K Q x   ♥ A K x x   ♦ K 10   ♣ K 10 x x

Bid two hearts. This is a maximum no-trump and a fine suit, but do not get ideas about the future of the hand. All you know at this stage is that you have been asked a question and that you have answered accurately.

66. ♠ Q J x x   ♥ A K x x   ♦ A J 10   ♣ K x

Bid two spades. If you have biddable suits in both majors, you begin by showing the spades—regardless of their comparative strength. Whenever your first rebid is in hearts, you state that you do not have biddable spades; but when your first rebid is in spades, there is a possibility that you also have hearts.

67. ♠ K 10 x   ♥ A x   ♦ A Q x x   ♣ K 10 x x

Bid two diamonds. You have no major suit, and your 18 points put you in the minimum range. It is coincidence that you have good diamonds; your partner cannot tell that your diamonds are really biddable.

68. ♠ K J x   ♥ Q J x   ♦ K x   ♣ A Q 10 x x

Bid two diamonds. You have no major suit, and your 18 points (including 1 point for the fifth club) put you in the minimum range. You do not have a real diamond suit, but you needn't worry. Your partner knows that your bid is artificial.

69. ♠ K J x   ♥ K x   ♦ Q x x   ♣ A K Q x x

Bid two no-trump. You have no major suit and your 19½ points put you in the maximum range. (Don't forget to count 1 point for length in a usable five-card suit.)

70. ♠ J x x x   ♥ J x x   ♦ A K x   ♣ A K Q

Bid two no-trump. This is an extreme example, since a no-trumper's four-card suit is usually biddable. In this case, the spades are *un*biddable. Even if partner has four spades, however, this hand may play better at no-trump.

Nature of Responder's Hand

The bidding has proceeded:

OPENER	RESPONDER
1 N-T	2 ♣

What sort of hand does the responder have?

He may have any of these five general types:

1. Very weak. He chooses to play the hand at three clubs rather than one no-trump.

2. Weak raise. 7½ to 9 points, usually with some hope for a major suit fit.

3. Sound raise. 9½ points or more, with or without ambitions in the major suits.

4. Any very strong hand, in which slam is a possibility.

5. 4-3-3-3 distribution and enough points to make a jump to four or more no-trump at the next turn.

As may be seen, the range goes all the way from part score to slam. For the most part the responder is in the driver's seat, since the opener has already told very nearly his full story in his opening bid and will tell a great deal more in his first rebid.

The responder must have very nearly full power to sign off at a part score contract; and he must be given the chance to make forcing bids without getting dangerously high. Thus he will have the maximum safety and flexibility, whether his hand is weak or strong.

The response of two clubs obliges both partners to keep the bidding open until they have reached two no-trump or three of a major.

Very Weak Hands

Your partner opens the bidding with one no-trump, and you have a long club suit in a nearly worthless hand. You have reason to believe that three clubs will be a better contract than one no-trump—even though three clubs may be doubled. With this sort of hand, you bid two clubs. At your next turn, you bid three clubs.

Requirements: A six-card or longer suit, most often with a singleton or void suit in the hand. (Without unbalanced distribution you would tend not to disturb one no-trump.) Fewer than $7\frac{1}{2}$ points, including one point each for the fifth and sixth clubs.

71. ♠ x ♥ x x ♦ x x x x ♣ Q 10 9 x x x

Bid two clubs. Even if your partner has only K-x in clubs, you should come close to making three clubs. At no-trump your hand may be quite worthless, and your partner may win only three or four tricks in all.

72. ♠ x ♥ x x ♦ K J x ♣ x x x x x x x

Bid two clubs. This hand will almost surely play better at three clubs than at one no-trump. However, if your partner, with a maximum no-trump and a fine club fit, should go on to three no-trump over your eventual rebid of three clubs, there should be a play for three no-trump.

73. ♠ x x ♥ K x ♦ x x x ♣ J 10 x x x x

Pass. One no-trump may be a fairly good contract.

There is no reason to believe that three clubs will be far better. The hand is much too weak, of course, to consider any other action. You will bid two clubs if one no-trump is doubled. Then the response would not be artificial, for you would redouble with a good hand; hence your bid must show weakness and a real club suit.

74. ♠ x x x x ♥ x ♦ x x ♣ K J x x x x

Bid two clubs. By coincidence, you have four-card support for a major suit. If your partner bids that major, you intend to pass! If he bids anything else, you will go to three clubs.

75. ♠ Q x x x ♥ x ♦ x x ♣ K J x x x x

Bid two clubs. If your partner bids two spades, you will raise to three spades. If he bids two hearts or two diamonds, you will go to three clubs. If he bids two no-trump, showing a maximum no-trump and no biddable major, you will bid a sporting three no-trump on the assumption that he can hold off the red suits long enough to develop and run nine tricks.

76. ♠ x x x x ♥ J x x x ♦ J x x x ♣ x

You may try a 'psychic' two-club bid. You are willing to pass the opener's rebid, no matter what it may be. If he bids two spades or two hearts, you have found a fit at a safe level. If he bids two diamonds, you must hope that he has four cards in the suit—highly probable when he cannot bid a major. If he bids two no-trump, you have made matters worse. It is not part of the Stayman Convention to bid two clubs on hands of this sort, but it's not the worst idea in the world by a long shot.

Incidentally, it would be a mistake to think that a

sign-off puts your partner into a strait-jacket. After you have bid two and three clubs, he knows that you have a limited hand but a club suit no worse than six to an honour. (If you have no high club, you should have some high card in a side suit.) If he has a maximum no-trump and a really good club fit, he may still take a chance on three no-trump. This is, however, unusual.

Two Clubs as a Weak Raise

When your partner opens the bidding with one no-trump, it is unsound to raise to two no-trump on a hand that counts less than 8 points. However, you may bid two clubs, instead of two no-trump, with only $7\frac{1}{2}$ points.

You are entitled to bid two clubs with $7\frac{1}{2}$ points only if you have good reason to look for a fit in a major suit. (You will not have good reason if your distribution, as responder, is 4-3-3-3 because then you have no ruffing power.)

77. ♠ K x x x ♥ Q J x x ♦ J 10 x x ♣ x

Bid two clubs. If your partner has a four-card major, you want to play the hand in that suit. If he has no four-card major, the hand will probably be played at two no-trump.

78. ♠ x ♥ K x x x ♦ Q J x x ♣ J 10 x x

Bid two clubs. This is a borderline case. If partner has a fit for hearts, there may be a play for game in that suit. Otherwise, even two no-trump may be in danger. Hence, if partner's rebid is two diamonds (showing a minimum no-trump), an unorthodox *pass* by you is a distinct possibility.

79. ♠ x x ♥ Q J x x x ♦ K 10 x x ♣ x x

Bid two clubs. There will be a play for game if partner has a maximum no-trump, especially if he has a good fit for hearts. This would be a better two-club bid if the black suits were 3-1 or if the hand contained as much as an additional ten. As it stands, it is another borderline case.

80. ♠ x   ♥ x x x   ♦ Q J x x x   ♣ K 10 x x

Bid two diamonds. The distribution is good, but there is no chance of finding a good fit in a major suit. Hence you cannot suggest strong action with only 7½ points. If partner has a maximum no-trump and good diamonds, he will bid again; otherwise, you are satisfied to play the hand at two diamonds.

81. ♠ x x   ♥ K x x x   ♦ A x x x   ♣ x x x

Pass. Your distribution is too poor for two clubs. You are quite satisfied to have your partner make a comfortable part score. With an additional jack you would take action, but the hand it as stands is too flimsy.

We have just seen that you are always interested in a major suit when you bid two clubs on a hand that counts only 7½ points. Is this also true of hands that count 8 to 9 points? Is it sound practice to bid two clubs with such hands when you are interested in a major suit, but two no-trump in all other cases?

No. That would be very unsound practice, because it would give a shrewd opponent an advantage on defence.

For example, suppose your shrewd opponent must make the opening lead when the bidding has been one, two, and three no-trump. He knows the dummy will seldom contain a four-card major. He will tend to lead a major suit whenever he has some sort of choice.

Or suppose that the bidding has been:

Opener	Responder
1 N-T	2 ♣
2 ♠	2 N-T
3 N-T	Pass

Your shrewd opponent knows (if you follow the practice just described) that you bid two clubs because you were interested in a major suit. You didn't like spades, so you must have hearts. Hence he shies away from a heart opening lead.

To avoid giving this information to your opponents, you must follow the practice of bidding two clubs rather than two no-trump even when you are not interested in a major suit.

Here is an example from actual play:

82.

NORTH
♠ Q 8 5
♥ 7 3
♦ J 8 4
♣ A 10 9 5 2

WEST
♠ 6
♥ Q 8 5 2
♦ 9 7 6 3 2
♣ K J 6

EAST
♠ J 9 7 3 2
♥ A 10 9 6 4
♦ K Q
♣ 4

SOUTH
♠ A K 10 4
♥ K J
♦ A 10 5
♣ Q 8 7 3

The bidding:

SOUTH	WEST	NORTH	EAST
1 N-T	Pass	2 ♣	Pass
2 ♠	Pass	2 N-T	Pass
3 N-T	Pass	Pass	Pass

The whole hand depended on West's opening lead. Should he pick the four-card major headed by the queen or the five-card minor headed by a spot card?

Perhaps West thought that the response of two clubs was more likely than not to show interest in a major suit. Whatever his mental process, he led a diamond, and South made the game without any trouble.

Now suppose that North (known to be playing the convention) has raised to two no-trump instead of bidding two clubs. South would have bid three no-trump, and West might well have led a heart.

Could North foresee all this when he bid two clubs? No. He didn't have to do any short-range prophesying. He simply bid two clubs on his way to two no-trump. It probably could do not harm, and it might do a lot of good.

The Raise to Two No-trump

As we have seen, responder bids two clubs when he has real interest in a major suit, and he also bids two clubs when he has no interest at all in a major suit. When does responder raise to two no-trump?

Responder raises to two no-trump when his hand counts $8\frac{1}{2}$ to 9 points and when he has no reason to look for a major-suit fit.

Let us see what opener can tell about responder's hand.

If responder raises immediately to two no-trump, he shows $8\frac{1}{2}$ to 9 points.

If responder bids two clubs and then goes to two no-trump at his second turn, he may have

(a) $7\frac{1}{2}$ to 9 points with disappointed hopes for a major-suit fit;

(b) 8 points without any expectation of a major-suit fit.

Now we can get back to the opener. He knows that he needs 27½ points to have an adequate play for game. If he is vulnerable, 27 points are enough.

If responder raises immediately to two no-trump, opener can go on to game with any maximum. The worst maximum is 19 points, and the worst responding hand will be 8½ points; so the total will be at least 27½ points.

If vulnerable, opener can go to game with 18½ points. The total will be at least 27 points. Opener may even bid three no-trump with 18½ points when not vulnerable or with 18 points when vulnerable if he feels like stretching.

However, opener does not get quite so gay if responder first bids two clubs and then bids two no-trump. Responder may have only 7½ or 8 points. Hence opener needs a full maximum (19 to 20 points) to go on to game.

What happens if responder has 8½ to 9 points with major-suit length that didn't strike a fit? Opener will, of course, still bid a game if he has a maximum. He will pass with 18½ points and may therefore occasionally fail to bid game when the combined count is 27½ points.

This is not really a great tragedy. A count of 27½ points will usually give you an adequate play for game, but not a guaranteed game. Hence you don't cry your eyes out if you occasionally stop short of game on such a hand.

83. ♠ J x x ♥ Q J x x ♦ K 10 x x ♣ 10 x

Bid two clubs. You have 8 points, and your partner may have 19½ or 20 points—in which case there will be a play for game. You are bidding two clubs as a sort of weak raise. You will take no further strong action with this hand.

84. ♠ J x x ♥ Q J x x ♦ K 10 x ♣ J 10 x

Bid two no-trump (not two clubs). With 9 points you are anxious to encourage opener to go on to game. The four-card heart suit is unimportant in view of your 4-3-3-3 distribution.

85. ♠ J 10 ♥ K 10 x x x ♦ Q J x x ♣ x x

Bid two clubs. You have hopes for this hand. If partner has a fit for hearts, you will play game in that suit. If he has a maximum no-trump without a heart fit, you won't worry too much about game at no-trump. If he has a minimum no-trump, the hand will be played at three hearts or two no-trump.

86. ♠ Q J x x ♥ Q J x x ♦ K x x x ♣ x

Bid two clubs. This is about the best hand you can have in this category. You have good distribution, a fit for either major and a full 9 points. If your partner has a four-card (or longer) major, you want to play at game in that suit. Otherwise, you are more anxious than not to go to game in no-trump.

87. ♠ K x x x ♥ K J x x x ♦ x x ♣ x x

Bid two clubs. If your partner has a maximum no-trump, the final contract will be four spades, four hearts, or three no-trump. If he has a minimum no-trump, the final contract will be three of a major or two no-trump.

Stopping Below Game

We know that the combined hands should have an adequate play for game if they contain 27½ points. What happens when the opening no-trump is based on $17\frac{1}{2}$ or 18 points and the responder has only $7\frac{1}{2}$ or 8 points?

In such situations, the partnership almost invariably stops short of game.

The opener knows that he has a minimum no-trump. He will avoid making any bid that he is not forced to make. The responder knows that his 8 points or so are not worth very much, and he also will avoid committing himself to game. Moreover, each of the partners will quickly realize that his partner has a minimum.

Is there any danger that one player will pass when his partner thought that a forcing situation existed? Not really. It's very easy to tell which bids are forcing and which are not forcing.

The response of two clubs is, of course, forcing. Assuming that responder's next bid is anything but three clubs, the two partners must keep the bidding open until a contract of two no-trump or three of a major is reached.

If the opener shows a maximum no-trump (by making a rebid of two no-trump), the partnership is headed for game. (The only exception is the case in which the responder's second bid is three clubs.) Both partners know about it, and no further forcing bids are necessary.

If the opener has but does not show a maximum at his first turn (that is, his rebid is two hearts or two spades), he may have to make a jump rebid later on to make sure of reaching game. Responder may have only $7\frac{1}{2}$ or 8 points, and the opener must show his strength to clarify the situation.

If the opener does not have a maximum, it is up to the responder to indicate whether or not he is interested in a game. If he bids in such a way as to commit himself only to two no-trump or three of a major, it will be assumed that he has a weak hand. If he makes any bid that doesn't directly lead to two no-trump or three of a major, it will be evident that he has a good hand. For example, he may bid three diamonds, etc.

In the illustrations that follow, the opener has a minimum no-trump and the responder has a weak hand. Note how the partnership exchanges information without getting too high.

Sequence 1

OPENER	RESPONDER	OPENER	RESPONDER
♠ A 10 x	♠ Q x x x	1 N-T	2 ♣
♥ K Q x	♥ J x x x	2 ♦	2 N-T
♦ K Q x x	♦ A x	Pass	
♣ Q J x	♣ x x x		

Opener shows a minimum no-trump and no biddable major suit. Responder was hoping for a fit in one of the majors or for a maximum no-trump. Since he is disappointed on both counts, he must indicate his weakness.

Opener naturally passes two no-trump. He has shown a minimum no-trump and the responder has shown no interest in reaching game.

Sequence 2

OPENER	RESPONDER	OPENER	RESPONDER
♠ A Q x	♠ x x	1 N-T	2 ♣
♥ x x x	♥ Q J x x x	2 ♦	2 ♥
♦ A Q x	♦ K 10 x x	2 N-T	Pass
♣ K Q 10 x	♣ x x		

Opener shows a minimum no-trump and no biddable major suit. Responder can afford to show the five-card heart suit since he doesn't need four-card support. He could not bid a four-card suit in this situation.

Opener is forced to bid, since the partnership is committed to two no-trump or three of a major. Opener would raise hearts with three headed by queen, king, or ace (or with four unbiddable hearts). Lacking such support, he bids two no-trump.

Sequence 3

OPENER	RESPONDER		OPENER	RESPONDER
♠ Q J x	♠ x x		1 N-T	2 ♣
♥ ⠀ x	♥ Q J x x x		2 ♦	2 ♥
♦ A	♦ ⠀o x x		3 ♥	Pass
♣ K Q J x	♣			

Opener shows his minim⠀⠀⠀⠀⠀⠀⠀⠀⠀⠀⠀⠀, and resp⠀⠀⠀⠀⠀ shows the hearts. Opener must raise, since he has th⠀⠀ to a high honour. He cannot raise to four hearts because he has announced a minimum no-trump and his partner is now captain of the hand.

Responder has a minimum and should pass at three hearts. Opener may have a hand that will produce a game, but this is very unlikely.

Sequence 4

OPENER	RESPONDER		OPENER	RESPONDER
♠ A x	♠ K x x x x		1 N-T	2 ♣
♥ J x x	♥ K x x x x		2 ♦	2 ♠
♦ K Q J x	♦ x x		2 N-T	3 ♥
♣ A Q x x	♣ x		Pass	

Opener shows his minimum, and responder trots out both of his major suits.

Note that no forcing situation exists, even though responder does quite a bit of bidding. He shows no willingness to get higher than three of a major, so the opener can pass with a clear conscience.

If responder had enough to insist on game he could jump to four hearts instead of bidding three hearts.

Sequence 5

OPENER	RESPONDER	OPENER	RESPONDER
♠ A J x	♠ K 10 x x	1 N-T	2 ♣
♥ K Q x x	♥ J x x	2 ♥	2 N-T
♦ K 10 x	♦ Q J x x	Pass	
♣ K J x	♣ 10 x		

Opener's first rebid shows a biddable heart suit and denies possession of biddable spades. Responder therefore knows that there is no fine fit in spades. With only 8 points, he must indicate his weakness and leave the rest to opener. Responder does not know the size of the opening no-trump.

Opener has a minimum no-trump and therefore has no reason to disturb the contract of two no-trump.

Sequence 6

OPENER	RESPONDER	OPENER	RESPONDER
♠ A J x	♠ x x	1 N-T	2 ♣
♥ K Q x x	♥ J 10 x x	2 ♥	3 ♥
♦ K 10 x	♦ A Q x	Pass	
♣ K J x	♣ x x x x		

Opener shows his hearts, as in the previous case. Responder raises to show four-card support. By raising to only three hearts, he shows a hand that is close to the minimum.

Responder could raise to four hearts to show a hand that was worth a game but not a slam. If responder had a little more than that, he could temporize with two spades or three diamonds, going to four hearts at his next turn.

Opener sees that both hands are limited, so passes.

Sequence 7

OPENER	RESPONDER	OPENER	RESPONDER
♠ A x x	♠ K J 10 x x	1 N-T	2 ♣
♥ K Q x x	♥ x x	2 ♥	2 ♠
♦ K J 10	♦ Q x x x	3 ♠	Pass
♣ K J x	♣ x x	—	—

Opener shows his hearts, as in the previous case. Responder can afford to show the spades, which are known to be at least five cards in length (since opener cannot have biddable spades).

Opener must raise with three to a high honour (queen, king, or ace) or with four unbiddable spades. Otherwise he bids no-trump. In either case, he would jump to show a maximum no-trump. Responder, with only $7\frac{1}{2}$ points, therefore passes under game.

Sequence 8

OPENER	RESPONDER	OPENER	RESPONDER
♠ x x x	♠ K 10 x x x	1 N-T	2 ♣
♥ K Q x x	♥ J x x	2 ♥	2 ♠
♦ K 10 x	♦ Q J x	2 N-T	Pass
♣ A K Q	♣ x x		

Opener shows his hearts and denies spades, as in the previous case. Responder shows the spades since opener may have a maximum no-trump and good support for a five-card spade suit.

Responder sees that the count is not enough to afford an adequate play for game, so he passes.

Sequence 9

OPENER	RESPONDER	OPENER	RESPONDER
♠ x x x	♠ Q J x x x x	1 N-T	2 ♣
♥ K Q 10 x	♥ x x	2 ♥	2 ♠
♦ Q J x	♦ K x	2 N-T	3 ♠
♣ A K Q	♣ x x x	Pass	

The bidding is like that of the previous case—up to the final bid of three spades. That shows a strong five-card suit, within the limits of a hand that is too weak for a jump to four spades, or (more likely) a six-card suit. Responder knows the opener has three small spades or a doubleton king or ace.

Opener can pass, since no forcing situation exists. However, opener might bid game with a minimum no-trump that consisted of more aces and kings (with fewer lower honours).

Reaching Game

Game will be reached when the opener has a maximum no-trump, when the responder has more than 9 points, or when a good fit can be established with slightly lesser values in the combined hands.

We have already noted that the opener may show his maximum at his first rebid or by a later jump. Responder may show adequate strength by a jump to game or by deviating from the path that leads to two no-trump or three of a major. In either case, a game is reached or a game-forcing situation is created.

These principles are illustrated in the sequences that follow.

Sequence 10

OPENER	RESPONDER	OPENER	RESPONDER
♠ A 10 x	♠ Q x x x	1 N-T	2 ♣
♥ K Q x	♥ J x x x	2 N-T	3 N-T
♦ K Q x x	♦ A x	Pass	
♣ K J 10	♣ x x x		

Opener shows a maximum no-trump without a biddable major suit. The hand must now be bid to game

—provided only that responder does not have the type of hand that calls for a sign-off in clubs (long clubs in a weak hand).

Responder has the weakest possible hand for a normal response of two clubs—7½ points. He must keep going, and since there is no major-suit fit, he goes to game in no-trump.

Sequence 11

OPENER	RESPONDER	OPENER	RESPONDER
♠ A x x	♠ K J 10 9 x	1 N-T	2 ♣
♥ K Q x	♥ x x	2 N-T	3 ♠
♦ K J 10	♦ Q x x x	4 ♠	Pass
♣ K Q x x	♣ x x		

Opener shows a maximum without a biddable major suit. Responder's spades are strong enough to play for game opposite strong three-card support, so he shows the suit.

Opener must raise with three spades to queen, king, or ace. With lesser support for spades, opener would go to three no-trump. (The hand must proceed to game since opener has shown a maximum.)

Compare with Sequence 7, where the partnership does not reach game.

Sequence 12

OPENER	RESPONDER	OPENER	RESPONDER
♠ x x x	♠ K J 10 9 x	1 N-T	2 ♣
♥ A Q x	♥ x x	2 N-T	3 ♠
♦ K 10 x	♦ Q x x x	3 N-T	Pass (or
♣ A K Q x	♣ x x		4 ♠)

The first four bids are the same as in Sequence 11. Opener cannot raise spades, so must go to three no-trump.

There is no guarantee that the game will be made, but there is a good play for it. The game would be quite easy if responder had slightly more than his dead minimum.

Sequence 13

OPENER	RESPONDER	OPENER	RESPONDER
A 10 x	♠ K J x x x	1 N-T	2 ♣
K Q 10 x	♥ x x	2 ♥	2 ♠
K J x	♦ Q 10 x x	4 ♠	Pass
K Q x	♣ x x		

Opener's first rebid shows biddable hearts, denies biddable spades, but does not show whether he has a minimum or a maximum no-trump. He shows his maximum with a jump bid at his next turn. Failure to jump would show a minimum, as in Sequence 7.

The play for game is slightly less than adequate. When you search for games that are hard to bid, you must expect to reach a few shaky contracts.

Sequence 14

OPENER	RESPONDER	OPENER	RESPONDER
♠ x x x	♠ K J x x x	1 N-T	2 ♣
K Q 10 x	♥ x x	2 ♥	2 ♠
A K J	♦ Q 10 x x	3 N-T	Pass
K Q 10	♣ x x		

The first four bids are the same as in Sequence 13, but then opener must jump to three no-trump. This shows a maximum no-trump without adequate spade support (Q-x-x or better). Compare with Sequence 8.

With good luck in hearts and clubs, the game will be made even against a bad spade break. If responder had a little more the play for game would be excellent.

Sequence 15

OPENER	RESPONDER	OPENER	RESPONDER
x x x	♠ Q J x x x x	1 N-T	2 ♣
A Q x x	♥ x x	2 ♥	2 ♠
A x x	♦ K x	2 N-T	3 ♠
A K x	♣ x x x	4 ♠	Pass

Opener first shows his hearts and then shows a minimum no-trump. Compare with Sequence 14.

Responder would now bid four spades or three no-trump with a strong hand (or could force with three diamonds or even three clubs). Three spades indicates weakness, but almost promises a six-card suit.

Opener is privileged to pass, but he can afford to go on since his values are in fast rather than in slow tricks. Compare with Sequence 9.

Sequence 16

OPENER	RESPONDER	OPENER	RESPONDER
A x x	♠ K x x x	1 N-T	2 ♣
K x x	♥ Q J x	2 ♦	3 N-T
K Q x	♦ J 10 x x	Pass	
A J x x	♣ Q x		

Opener shows a minimum no-trump with no biddable major suit. Now it is up to responder to show whether or not he has the values for game. With 9½ points, he can afford to bid game. The combined total will be 27 points if opener has a dead minimum, and may be as high as 28 points.

Compare with Sequence 1, where the partnership does not reach game.

Sequence 17

Opener	Responder	Opener	Responder
♠ A x x	♠ Q x x x x	1 N-T	2 ♣
♥ Q J x	♥ K x x	2 ♦	2 ♠
♦ K Q 10 x	♦ x x x	3 ♠	3 N-T
♣ A 10 x	♣ K J	Pass	

Opener's first rebid shows a minimum no-trump without a biddable major suit. Responder is now in doubt: he has 9 points in high cards, and doesn't know whether or not to count anything for spade length.

When opener can raise spades, responder can risk a game bid. No-trump is better than spades, since it may be makable even if spades break badly. If opener had denied a spade fit by bidding two no-trump, responder would have passed.

Sequence 18

Opener	Responder	Opener	Responder
♠ A J x	♠ K x x x x	1 N-T	2 ♣
♥ Q J x	♥ K x x	2 ♦	2 ♠
♦ A Q x	♦ x	3 ♠	4 ♠
♣ Q J x x	♣ K x x	Pass	

Opener shows a minimum no-trump without a biddable major. Responder shows a five-card spade suit, and opener raises to show Q-x-x or better. The spade fit now increases responder's count to 10 points, and he can bid game. Since he has a singleton, he prefers spades to no-trump. Compare with Sequence 17.

Sequence 19

Opener	Responder	Opener	Responder
♠ A x x	♠ K x x	1 N-T	2 ♣
♥ Q J x x	♥ x x x x	2 ♥	4 ♥
♦ K Q 10	♦ A x	Pass	
♣ A 10 x	♣ Q J x x		

Opener's rebid shows biddable hearts but does not show whether his no-trump is minimum or maximum. Responder has enough to insist on game but knows there is no slam. (35 points are needed for slam, and responder's $10\frac{1}{2}$ points opposite a maximum no-trump will come to only $30\frac{1}{2}$ points.)

Compare with Sequence 6.

Sequence 20

OPENER	RESPONDER	OPENER	RESPONDER
♠ A K x x	♠ Q 10	1 N-T	2 ♣
♥ A J 10 x	♥ Q x x x	2 ♠	3 ♦
♦ Q x x	♦ A J x x x	3 ♥	4 ♥
♣ K x	♣ x x	Pass	

Opener shows biddable spades. Responder can insist on game since he has 11 points (including diamond length). Three diamonds is forcing to game since it cannot be intended to lead directly to two no-trumps or three of a major.

Opener now shows hearts, and responder raises. If opener had no biddable hearts, he would bid three no-trump, and responder would pass.

This hand was held in the 1950 Summer Championships, as described on page 18.

Sequence 21

OPENER	RESPONDER	OPENER	RESPONDER
♠ A Q x x	♠ K 10	1 N-T	2 ♣
♥ K Q x	♥ J x x x x	2 ♠	2 N-T
♦ K x	♦ x x x	3 ♣	3 ♥
♣ A J x x	♣ K x x	4 ♥	Pass

Opener shows biddable spades, and responder shows a minimum by bidding two no-trump. Since opener has a maximum, he can afford to go to game.

76

Opener can afford to make the waiting bid of three clubs to give responder the chance to show a five-card heart suit. If he chose, opener could bid three diamonds to confuse the enemy.

Responder seizes the chance, and game in hearts is reached.

Sequence 22

OPENER	RESPONDER	OPENER	RESPONDER
♠ K Q x x	♠ x	1 N-T	2 ♣
♥ x x x	♥ K J 10 x x	2 ♠	3 ♥
♦ A Q x	♦ K x x	3 N-T	Pass
♣ A Q 10	♣ J x x x		

Opener shows biddable spades, and responder forces to game by bidding three hearts. If responder could not insist on game, he would bid two no-trump. He would get a chance to show his hearts if opener had a maximum (as in Sequence 21).

Responder cannot afford to bid two no-trump, for opener would pass with a minimum. This is all implied by his bid of three hearts.

Bidding Slams

Perhaps you have noticed that many of the game contracts just recommended would be hard to play. This is not a coincidence.

I have already mentioned that there should be an 'adequate' play for game when the combined hands count to $27\frac{1}{2}$ points. You'll make the game about half of the time with such a count. With one extra point, you'll make game far more often and with much more comfort. With 29 or more points game is a near-certainty.

Since this is a book on 'expert' bidding, I haven't bothered much with examples of games that any beginner can bid. The expert gets as many comfortable games as the beginner; but his chief bidding advantage lies rather in the hands where it is touch and go whether game should be bid.

Much the same principle applies to slam bidding. An experienced player can ordinarily avoid a slam for which there is no conceivable play; and he can always bid a slam in which there are tricks to burn. The chief bidding advantage of the expert lies in reaching slams for which the play is barely 'adequate' and in avoiding slams for which the play is slightly less than adequate.

In this connection we may note again that the play for small slam is adequate if you have an even chance to make it. For a grand slam you want favourable odds of 2 to 1.

When both of the partnership hands contain balanced distribution, a count of 35 points should provide an adequate play for a small slam; a count of 39 points, for a grand slam.

When one of the partnership hands is unbalanced, slam in a suit may be made with a lower count. If there is no duplication of values, a small slam should be considered when the count is:

(a) 31 points (with a singleton); or
(b) 27 points (with a void suit).

The difficulty with such hands is to find out whether or not there is duplication. If your singleton or void is opposite your partner's strongest suit, you may need the full normal count of 35 points for the slam. If your short suit is opposite your partner's weakest suit, you will need fewer points for the slam.

When the bidding has been opened with one no-trump, the proper way to reach a touch-and-go slam will vary with the distribution of the responder. If responder has a flat hand, the slam will depend on sheer power; and he need only find out the exact size of the no-trump. If responder has a long suit but no singleton or void, the slam will depend on fit as well as on power; and he must do some exploring. If responder has a singleton or void, the slam will depend partly on the extent of duplication; and he must bid with great delicacy.

Because these three situations call for different treatment we will discuss them separately. However, many remarks made in one discussion will apply to the others.

Don't forget that in slam bidding the tens are given no point value. But tens have value and should be considered.

Sheer Power

When the responder has 4-3-3-3 distribution, he knows that the slam will depend on sheer power. The combined count should be 35 points for a small slam; 39 points for a grand slam. The opening bid shows $17\frac{1}{2}$ to 20 points, and responder must supply the rest.

Responder can show the count of his hand by:

(a) a jump to 4 N-T, 5 N-T, 6 N-T, or 7 N-T; or

(b) a bid of two clubs, followed immediately by a jump to four or more no-trump.

The exact count shown by responder varies according to the particular jump or combination-bid that he selects. This can be summarized in the following table (which need not be memorized):

Response	Responder's Count
4 N-T	$15\frac{1}{2}$ to 16
2 ♣ and 4 N-T	$16\frac{1}{2}$ to 17
5 N-T	$17\frac{1}{2}$ to 18
2 ♣ and 5 N-T	$18\frac{1}{2}$ to 19
6 N-T	$19\frac{1}{2}$ to 20
2 ♣ and 6 N-T	$20\frac{1}{2}$ to 21
7 N-T	$21\frac{1}{2}$ or more

You may need this table once in a year or so, depending on how often you play and what sort of cards you tend to hold. When you need the table, you can reconstruct it mentally in a few seconds.

Just remember the nature of the table. Each bid has a count of a certain number or of $\frac{1}{2}$ point less than that. A response of two clubs combined with a jump to four no-trump is considered stronger than an immediate jump to four no-trump; and likewise with the higher bids.

All you need is a starting point, from which you can work it all out. The easiest starting point is the jump to seven no-trump. That must guarantee a combined total of 39 points opposite a dead minimum no-trump ($17\frac{1}{2}$ points). Hence the jump to seven no-trump must show at least $21\frac{1}{2}$ points. The next weaker bid must show $20\frac{1}{2}$ to 21; the one below that must show $19\frac{1}{2}$ to 20; and so on.

Each of these bids or combinations either asks a question or tells a story. The opener notes the count shown by responder, adds his own count, and takes the action suggested by the total.

Opener	Responder
1 N-T	4 N-T
?	

Responder shows 15½ or 16 points. Opener passes with a minimum no-trump. He bids six no-trump with 19½ or 20 points, because then the count is surely at least 35 points. Opener bids five no-trump with 19 points, because the combined count is then either 34½ or 35 points. Responder bids six with 16 points but passes with 15½ points.

Opener	Responder
1 N-T	2 ♣
2 ♠	4 N-T

Responder shows 16½ or 17 points. Opener passes with a dead minimum of 17½ points. He bids six no-trump with 18½ points or more, because then the combined count is at least 35 points (and at most only 37 points). He bids five no-trump with 18 points, inviting responder to go on to six if he has 17 points.

Opener	Responder
1 N-T	5 N-T
?	

Responder shows 17½ or 18 points. The combined total will be 35 points to 38 points. Hence the opener must always bid six but never seven.

Opener	Responder
1 N-T	2 ♣
2 ♠	5 N-T
?	

Responder shows 18½ or 19 points. The combined total will be 39 points only if the opener has an absolute

F   81

maximum of 20 points opposite a responder who has 19 points. Opener may show an absolute maximum by bidding six of any new suit. Responder will then bid six no-trump with $18\frac{1}{2}$ points; seven no-trump, with 19 points. If opener has less than an absolute maximum he simply bids six no-trump.

OPENER	RESPONDER
1 N-T	6 N-T
?	

Responder shows $19\frac{1}{2}$ to 20 points. Opener bids seven no-trump with $19\frac{1}{2}$ or 20 points of his own. With less, opener passes.

OPENER	RESPONDER
1 N-T	2 ♣
2 ♠	6 N-T
?	

Responder shows $20\frac{1}{2}$ or 21 points. Opener bids seven no-trump with $18\frac{1}{2}$ points or more; but passes with $17\frac{1}{2}$ or 18 points.

Effect of Opener's Rebid

When responder bids two clubs, the opener sometimes shows by his rebid the size of his no-trump. This has very little effect on the type of bidding we have been discussing.

If the opener's rebid is two diamonds, showing a minimum, responder carries on with his original plan. That is, responder jumps to four no-trump with $16\frac{1}{2}$ or 17 points; to five no-trump, with $18\frac{1}{2}$ or 19 points; and to six no-trump, with $20\frac{1}{2}$ or 21 points. Opener then passes or continues depending on the combined count.

If the opener's rebid is two no-trump, showing a

maximum, responder bids one trick higher in no-trump than he had originally planned. With 16½ or 17 points, he jumps to five no-trump (instead of four). With 18½ or 19 points, he jumps to six no-trump (instead of five). With 20½ or 21 points, he jumps to seven no-trump (instead of six). The opener counts the points in the combined hands and takes whatever action is indicated.

Exploration

When the responder has some balanced distribution other than 4-3-3-3, he must consider the advantages of fitting suits and long suits. There may be a better play for the slam in a fitting suit, if that fit can be discovered. In other situations, a slam may be bid with less than the normal count, but with suit length as compensation.

Here we must take time out to discuss the effect of suit length on expert slam bidding.

When neither of the partnership hands contains a long suit (five or more cards) or a short suit (singleton or void), great respect must be paid to aces and kings. You cannot afford to bid a slam if the opponents can hold as much as an ace and a king against you.

For example, let us return to the hand shown on page 26:

88

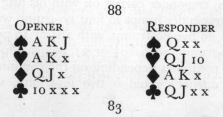

OPENER	RESPONDER
♠ A K J	♠ Q x x
♥ A K x	♥ Q J 10
♦ Q J x	♦ A K x
♣ 10 x x x	♣ Q J x x

Most point-count players (including experts as well as average players) would reach six no-trump. Opener would bid one no-trump, and responder would show 15 points (Work count) by jumping to four no-trump.

Opener, with 18 points (Work count) would accept the invitation by proceeding to six. The combined count would be 33 points, which is considered adequate in the most popular point-count systems, based on this count.

The slam would fail no matter which suit was led. There are no long suits to furnish discards in the happy event that the defenders fail to take their tricks in a hurry.

We might note, in passing, that this little mishap could not happen to those who use my corrected count. The opening bid is one no-trump, and the response is four no-trump; but then precision takes over. Opener has 19 points and knows that responder has 15½ or 16 points. He proceeds to five no-trump, leaving the decision up to responder. That player would bid six with 16 points, but must pass with only 15½ points.

The situation would be treated differently if either hand contained a five-card suit. Then there might be a reasonable play for twelve tricks even if the opponents held an ace and a king.

To begin with, the ace and king might be in different suits, and a finesse might shut out the king. Secondly, the defenders might fail to cash even if the ace-king were in the same suit; and then the long suit might provide enough tricks. Finally, the defenders might not really have an ace and a king; they might have two kings and a queen, or some such values.

For example:

89.

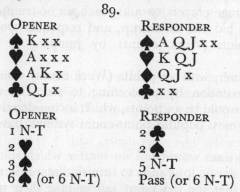

OPENER	RESPONDER
♠ K x x	♠ A Q J x x
♥ A x x x	♥ K Q J
♦ A K x	♦ Q J x
♣ Q J x	♣ x x

OPENER	RESPONDER
1 N-T	2 ♣
2 ♥	2 ♠
3 ♠	5 N-T
6 ♠ (or 6 N-T)	Pass (or 6 N-T)

Responder has a count of $17\frac{1}{2}$ points, counting 1 point for the length in spades. Opener's raise to three spades shows K-x-x with a minimum no-trump. Hence responder can count 35 to 36 points in the combined hands—of which 1 point is for spade length. The opponents may have an ace and a king. In fact, they *do*.

Responder nevertheless takes his chances. He bids five no-trump to offer a choice of slams. Perhaps opener has the king of clubs and will benefit by having the opening lead come to him.

The slam is made if the defenders fail to take their top clubs immediately. This is not a very good contract, but any expert would be quite happy if he never reached a worse slam.

The point is that if you try to stay out of such slams, you will also miss many perfectly sound slam contracts. For example, opener might have:

90.   ♠ K x x   ♥ A x x x   ♦ A x x   ♣ K Q J

If diamonds are led, the finesse must be taken. Otherwise, there are twelve cold tricks. At six no-trump the slam is unbeatable.

To make the case even stronger, opener might have:

91. ♠ K x x   ♥ A x x x   ♦ K x x   ♣ A K x

There are twelve cold tricks at spades or no-trump, regardless of the defence.

Grand slams are a slightly different story. It's all right to consider length, but it is risky to count more than 1 point for a long suit. That would make it possible for you to bid a grand slam with 38 points in high cards. The opponents, with 4 points, could not have an ace.

Mind you, I wouldn't criticize a player who counted more than 1 point for a long, solid suit. He might find an ace out against him, but the chances would be all in his favour. That is, the outstanding points might not be an ace; or, if it were an ace, it might not be taken at once.

I point this out only so that you may know what risks are involved if you bid a grand slam with a long suit as its backbone.

When the responder has 4-4-3-2 distribution, he can count nothing for length. He will try to determine whether or not the combined count is at least 35 points (or, for a grand slam, 39 points). At the same time he will try to find a fit for one of his four-card suits.

Sequence 23

OPENER	RESPONDER	OPENER	RESPONDER
♠ A Q x	♠ K J x x	1 N-T	2 ♣
♥ A J x x	♥ Q x x	2 ♥	2 ♠
♦ K x x	♦ A x	3 ♠	4 ♣
♣ K x x	♣ A Q x x	4 ♠	4 N-T
		5 N-T	6 N-T
		Pass	

Responder has 17 points and wants to reach a slam unless opener has a dead minimum. Responder bids two spades only to discover the size of the no-trump—not to show a suit. Opener shows a minimum no-trump by the raise to three spades, whereupon responder can invite the slam (first trying for a club fit). When responder bids four no-trump, in the full knowledge that opener has $17\frac{1}{2}$ to $18\frac{1}{2}$ points, opener can afford to think well of an 18-point hand. With $18\frac{1}{2}$ points, he would jump to six spades, which responder would take back to six no-trump.

Sequence 24

Opener	Responder	Opener	Responder
♠ K 7 4	♠ A 8 5 2	1 N-T	2 ♣
♥ A K 6	♥ J 4	2 N-T	3 ♦
♦ A Q 9 2	♦ K 10 6 3	3 N-T	5 N-T
♣ Q 9 3	♣ A K 10	6 ♦	Pass

This hand, played in a team match, found one team going down at six no-trump while the other team made the far superior contract of six diamonds.

Responder with 16 points is willing to bid a slam as soon as opener shows a maximum no-trump. He first shows the diamonds and then offers a choice of slams by jumping to five no-trump. Opener can then show support for the diamonds, and the slam is played there.

Note that opener bids three no-trump despite the diamond fit, having already shown a maximum no-trump.

Sequence 25

Opener	Responder	Opener	Responder
♠ K 10 x	♠ A J x	1 N-T	2 ♣
♥ A Q x x	♥ K x x x	2 ♥	2 ♠
♦ K Q x	♦ A x	4 ♠	6 ♥
♣ A x x	♣ Q J x x	Pass	

Again responder has 16 points and wants to bid a slam if opener has a maximum. Opener's rebid does not show the size of the no-trump, so responder bids spades merely to find out. The jump to four spades shows a maximum no-trump, so responder proceeds at once to six hearts.

If opener had shown a minimum no-trump by raising to only three spades, responder would have made a slam try but could not insist on a slam.

It is important to notice that the responder can often find out what he wants to know without getting past game. A hand may be played for game or for slam, but rarely for five of a major or five no-trump.

Much the same principles are employed when responder has a five-card suit. He bids in such a way as to determine the size of the no-trump and the possibility of a suit fit.

Sequence 26

OPENER	RESPONDER	OPENER	RESPONDER
♠ K Q J x	♠ A x	1 N-T	2 ♣
♥ K J x	♥ A Q 10 x x	2 ♠	3 ♥
♦ K x x	♦ J x x	4 ♣	5 N-T
♣ A Q x	♣ K x x	6 N-T	Pass

Responder counts 16 points, including 1 point for heart length. He wants to reach a slam if opener has a maximum no-trump. As we saw in Sequence 22, the bid of three hearts is forcing.

Opener shows a maximum and a heart fit by bidding four clubs. Responder offers a choice of slams by bidding five no-trump, and opener gladly goes to six no-trump to avoid a diamond opening through his king.

Sequence 27

OPENER	RESPONDER	OPENER	RESPONDER
K J x	♠ A x	1 N-T	2 ♣
K x	♥ A Q x x x	2 ♦	2 ♥
A 10 x x	♦ K Q x x	2 N-T	3 ♦
♣ K Q 10 x	♣ x x	3 N-T	4 N-T
		5 ♦	6 ♦
		Pass	

Responder counts 17 points, including 1 point for heart length. He wants to reach a slam if some good fit can be found.

He shows strong slam ambitions by bidding four no-trump. Opener must show his fine fit for diamonds, particularly since he has an excellent heart holding.

Sequence 28

OPENER	RESPONDER	OPENER	RESPONDER
K Q 8	♠ A 3	1 N-T	2 ♣
A K 8 4	♥ Q 7 5	2 ♥	4 ♣
K J 7	♦ A Q 2	5 N-T	7 N-T
K 8 3	♣ A Q 10 9 5	Pass	

(This hand was dealt in the World Championship Match at Bermuda, 1950. I was opener; Howard Schenken, responder.)

Responder shows strong slam interest by going past three no-trump. Opener shows that his no-trump is a maximum by jumping to five no-trump. (Opener would probably find some other bid without a good club fit; and would bid a non-committal four no-trump with a minimum.) Responder can read the message clearly and can count a total of at least 39 points.

Actually, Schenken was using the Four-Aces Count,

from which much has been borrowed in the development of the system recommended in this book. The bidding in both counts is identical.

Unbalanced Hands

We have discussed slam bidding with balanced hands indicating how the two partners arrive at the combined count and at the same time find the best fit. If some of the slam contracts look a bit uncomfortable, it is your privilege to raise the slam requirements by a point or so.

Unbalanced hands will tend to produce a cleavage between the bold and the conservative. It is not always possible to find out to what extent a singleton is duplicated by partner's high cards in the same suit. The bold player may take a chance anyway; the conservative player will not.

We have already arrived at a figure of 31 points for a small slam when one hand contains a singleton; 27 points, when it is void of a suit. These figures are based on the assumption that there is no serious duplication.

This means that responder begins to consider the possibility of a slam when he has upwards of 11 points if his hand contains a singleton; or with upwards of 7 points if he is void of a suit. Those are extreme cases, of course, since slam will be bid only if the no-trump is a maximum and is weak in responder's short suit.

Not every such slam can be bid. However, most players bid practically none of them with their ordinary bidding methods—largely because they do not see the possibilities until the dummy has appeared on the table.

In the examples that follow, responder takes strong action with rather skimpy hands. Conservative players might require another point or two for similar action.

The reader is referred also, for examples of exploring for duplication, to the four sequences on pages 96–98.

Sequence 29

OPENER	RESPONDER	OPENER	RESPONDER
♠ A x x	♠ K Q x x x x	1 N-T	2 ♣
♥ K x x	♥ x	2 N-T	3 ♠
♦ A J x	♦ K Q x x	4 ♠	5 ♦
♣ A Q x x	♣ x x	5 N-T	6 ♠
			Pass

Responder counts 12 points, including 2 points for spade length. He knows that the combined count is at least 31 points as soon as opener shows a maximum. He tries to find out about duplication by bidding five diamonds.

Opener has help for diamonds and fast tricks in all suits. He therefore accepts the invitation by bidding five no-trump; and responder goes to six spades.

Sequence 30

OPENER	RESPONDER	OPENER	RESPONDER
♠ A x x	♠ K Q x x x x	1 N-T	2 ♣
♥ K J x	♥ x	2 N-T	3 ♠
♦ A J x	♦ K Q x x	4 ♠	5 ♦
♣ K Q x x	♣ x x	5 ♠	Pass

Responder has the same hand as in Sequence 29, and bids it in similar fashion. Opener must show less enthusiasm when responder bids five diamonds.

Opener has only 19 points and could not have less for the maximum no-trump that he has already shown. Moreover, he has only two aces. He must sign off at five spades, leaving it up to responder to proceed.

Responder naturally gives up the idea of bidding a slam.

CHAPTER VII

Encouraging Responses to One No-trump

The Raise to Two No-trump

The raise to two no-trump is made on a hand that contains:

(a) *Strength:* 8½ to 9 points.

(b) *Distribution:* No length in a major suit, except when the distribution is 4-3-3-3. Otherwise the distribution may be balanced or mildly unbalanced.

89. ♠ K x x   ♥ J x x   ♦ Q x x   ♣ Q 10 x x

Bid two no-trump. This is a balanced hand with 8½ points and no support for a four-card major suit.

90. ♠ x x   ♥ K x x   ♦ K x x x   ♣ K x x x

Bid two no-trump. This is your maximum holding for such a bid. With even one additional ten-spot you could jump to three no-trump.

91. ♠ x x   ♥ x x x   ♦ Q J x x x   ♣ K J x

Bid two clubs (not two no-trump). Counting 1 point for length in diamonds, the hand comes to only 8 points.

92. ♠ K x x x   ♥ x x   ♦ K x x x   ♣ K x x

Bid two clubs (not two no-trump). If the opener has

biddable spades, you are interested in a spade contract. You would have no such interest with 4-3-3-3 distribution, but you do with 4-4-3-2.

The Opener's Rebid

The bidding has proceeded:

OPENER	RESPONDER
1 N-T	2 N-T
?	

What should the opener do?

He adds his own points to the 8½ or 9 points shown by the responder. Thus he finds the combined total. Then he acts on the following basis:

When the combined total is 27½ or more, he bids game. If vulnerable, he bids game with a combined count of only 27 points.[1]

To be specific, opener always bids three no-trump with a maximum opening bid of one no-trump (19 to 20 points). When vulnerable, he bids three no-trumps even with only 18½ points.

When a hand includes several eights or nines, those cards may be estimated as being worth one ten-spot. Hence, opener may even go on to game with an 18-point hand that is rich in high spot-cards. (If the bidding takes a slammish turn, this extra value is disregarded—just as the value of ten-spots is always disregarded in slam bidding.)

___

[1] The value of a part score remains the same, regardless of vulnerability; but a vulnerable game is worth more than a non-vulnerable game. Therefore you can afford to stretch just the merest trifle more for a vulnerable than for a non-vulnerable game.

The Raise to Three No-trump

The raise to three no-trump is made on a hand that contains:

> *Minimum:* 9½ points ⎫ balanced
> *Maximum:* not enough for a slam ⎬ distribution

The minimum of 9½ points explains itself, but the maximum requirement needs a word or two. There will be a reasonable play for slam if the combined hands add up to 35 points without counting ten-spots. The responder must add his own points to his partner's possible points to make sure that the combined total is less than what is needed for a slam.

Suppose the opener has his maximum of 20 points. The responder may have 14½ points without counting tens, provided that his distribution is 4-3-3-3. The combined total will come to no more than 34½ points; and it will be less if the opener doesn't have a maximum. There is no harm in playing such a hand at three no-trump without exploring slam possibilities.

However, as the responding hand gets close to 14½ points, he should tend to bid two clubs instead of jumping to three no-trump, particularly if he has any distribution but 4-3-3-3. Then the bidding may reveal a 4-4 fit, or complete solidification of some long suit. When the combined hands are so close to the slam quota, any such revelation may justify a slam bid.

As the responding hand gets close to the minimum level (9½ points, he should tend to bid three no-trump rather than two clubs unless the hand has good support for a four-card major suit. If slam is out of the question, bid three no-trump and don't tell the enemy a thing.

Even this principle has its exceptions. With certain hands you can plan to confuse the enemy without disturbing your partner, and your first step is to bid two clubs. This point will be more fully developed in the examples which follow :

93. ♠ A x x ♥ x x x ♦ K x x ♣ Q x x x

Bid three no-trump (or two clubs). This is the minimum holding for a jump to three no-trump.

94. ♠ A Q x ♥ K x x ♦ K x x ♣ Q x x x

Bid three no-trump (or two clubs). This is the maximum holding for a jump to three no-trump (14½ points). If the distribution were anything but 4-3-3-3, a response of two clubs would be preferred.

95. ♠ Q J 10 ♥ x x ♦ K x x x x ♣ K Q J

Bid three no-trump (or two clubs). This is the maximum holding when the responding hand has a five-card suit. A response of two clubs would be preferred if the diamonds were longer or stronger, or if the hand contained a singleton. There is a chance to reach a delicate slam if your first response is two clubs; there is no chance at all if you jump to three no-trump (since opener must pass).

96. ♠ x x ♥ x x ♦ K Q x x x x ♣ A x x

Bid three no-trump (or two clubs). This is the maximum holding when the responding hand has a good six-card suit. A response of two clubs would be preferred if the major suits were 3-1, or if the distribution were improved in any other way.

97. ♠ x x x x ♥ Q x x ♦ A J x x ♣ Q x

Bid two clubs (*not* three no-trump). If the opener can bid two spades, you will raise to four spades. Otherwise, you will go to three no-trump.

98. ♠ x ♥ x x x ♦ A Q x x x ♣ Q x x x

Bid two clubs (*not* three no-trump). If opener bids two spades, you can jump to three no-trump with some assurance that the most dangerous lead has been stopped. If opener bids two no-trump, you can raise to three no-trump and depend on sheer power to see you through. If opener bids two hearts, you will jump to three no-trump and hope that the opening leader will shy away from spades on the assumption that you are interested in a major suit. If opener bids two diamonds, you can bid two spades yourself! At worst, opener can raise to three spades (he cannot pass); and then you can go to three no-trump. This psychic bid can do no harm and may well stop a spade lead.

99. ♠ — ♥ x x x ♦ K Q J x x x ♣ A x x x

Bid two clubs (*not* three no-trump). Five or even six diamonds may be a better contract than three no-trump. There can be no harm in exploring the possibilities. The bidding may develop in a number of different ways, of which the following four are the most interesting.

Sequence 31

Opener	Responder
1 N-T	2 ♣
2 N-T	3 ♦
3 ♠	3 N-T
Pass	

The opener's rebid shows a maximum no-trump without a biddable major suit. Responder would simply bid three no-trump unless he needed further information, so his actual bid of three diamonds logically asks opener to tell more. Opener, in this case, shows strength in spades (but has already denied a biddable major, so cannot have a four-card spade suit). This is the re-assurance that responder needs, so he proceeds to three no-trump.

Sequence 32

OPENER	RESPONDER
1 N-T	2 ♣
2 N-T	3 ♦
3 ♥	3 ♠ !

The responder will eventually play the hand at diamonds. The less opener likes the spades, the more responder will tend towards bidding a slam; and vice versa. Instead of bidding three spades, the responder might cue-bid at four clubs or might jump to five diamonds. Different partnerships may prefer different methods, but any pair of experts will surely note with interest how much information can be obtained.

Sequence 33

OPENER	RESPONDER
1 N-T	2 ♣
2 ♦	2 ♠
3 ♠	3 N-T
Pass	

Responder makes a psychic spade bid, knowing that the opener (who has already announced a minimum no-trump) cannot raise to more than three spades. Now responder can bid three no-trump with some assurance of having stopped a spade lead—since his bidding could be quite legitimate. Even if spades are led (by a very suspicious player), opener has shown three to a high honour in the suit and can stop the suit.

Sequence 34

OPENER	RESPONDER
1 N-T	2 ♣
2 ♦	2 ♠
2 N-T	5 ♦
Pass or 6 ♦	

Opener first shows a minimum no-trump without a biddable major suit. Then, by failing to raise spades, he shows less than Q-x-x-, K-x-x, or A-x-x in that suit. Opener's strength must be where it can do the most good, and responder suggests a slam by jumping at once to five diamonds. Opener will go to six diamonds with a good diamond fit and a count of 18 or 18½ points, provided that his count does not include ten-spots.

For example, opener will bid six diamonds with any of the following hands:

100. ♠ J 10 x   ♥ A Q x   ♦ A x x x   ♣ K Q J
101. ♠ J x x   ♥ A K x   ♦ A x x x   ♣ K Q x
102. ♠ K x x   ♥ A Q x   ♦ A x x x   ♣ K J 10

The Opener's Rebid

The bidding has proceeded:

OPENER	RESPONDER
1 N-T	3 N-T
?	

What should the opener do?

He must pass. There are no exceptions to this rule.

The Jump to Three or Four of a Suit

The responder jumps to three of a major suit when he wants to bid a game *but not a slam*, and when there is

98

some question in his mind as to the best final contract. His choice may be between four of his major and three no-trump, or between four spades and four hearts. (If there is no question in his mind, he should bid four of his major suit or three no-trump immediately.)

It follows that the responder has a five-card or six-card suit. With a seven-card suit, he would either bid game at once or two clubs to explore slam possibilities (depending on the strength of his hand).

The responder must have a minimum of $9\frac{1}{2}$ points, including the count for length in his suit. His maximum is determined by the principles already discussed in the response of three no-trump. That is, he must not have so much that slam is a likelihood. The jump to three says that slam is not to be considered.

The jump to three of a minor is rare. If the responding hand is strong enough to play for five diamonds or five clubs, and too unbalanced to play at three no-trump, slam is at least a possibility. A first response of two clubs will lead to better results with such hands.

The jump to four of a major is made with a six-card or seven-card suit when slam is quite out of the question. If the count for length is disregarded, the point value of the hand is always very low—about 3 to 8 points. It is often a gambling bid.

The jump to five of a minor does not exist (except for some freak hand that you will probably never hold). If the hand is poor in high cards, responder should gamble in three no-trump rather than in five of a minor. If the hand is fairly strong, slam is a possibility; and responder should explore with a bid of two clubs.

103. ♠ A x ♥ K Q x x x x ♦ x x x ♣ x x

Bid three hearts (or two clubs). With even slightly

greater strength, or even with better distribution (such as 6-4-2-1), slam would become a possibility. With the actual hand, your choice is between four hearts and three no-trump.

104. ♠ A Q J x x x ♥ x x ♦ x x x ♣ x x

Bid three spades. You are willing to pass three no-trump, but first you show a major suit that needs very little help.

105. ♠ x x ♥ x ♦ A Q J x x x ♣ K x x x

Bid two clubs (*not* three diamonds). A slam is possible, and responder should set out on an exploring trip.

106. ♠ 10 9 x x x x ♥ x x ♦ A x ♣ Q x x

Bid two clubs (*not* three spades). You have 7 points in high cards and a doubtful 2 points for length in spades. You are not sure that the combined hands count to $27\frac{1}{2}$ points, and you are not sure of a spade fit. Hence you do not force to game; you allow for a chance to play the hand at less than game.

107. ♠ Q J 10 x x ♥ Q J 10 x x ♦ x ♣ Q x

Bid three spades. If opener goes to three no-trump, your next bid should be four hearts. The jump to three of a suit indicates that you have a choice—in this case between four spades and four hearts.

108. ♠ x ♥ K Q J x x x ♦ J x x x ♣ Q x

Bid four hearts. There is no choice with this hand; you want a final contract of four hearts. Slam is conceivable, but too unlikely to be taken seriously.

109. ♠ K x x x x x x ♥ x x ♦ x x x ♣ x

Bid four spades. You can't tell how many tricks you will win, but must gamble on game with this sort of hand. Scientific bidding will not help you with freak hands; you must decide for yourself whether or not to go to game.

Wholesale Slam Conventions

Like most American bridge players, we use the Blackwood Convention in absolutely clear-cut situations to check on aces. When the bidding has been opened in no-trump, any later bid of four or five no-trump is *not* a Blackwood bid in our view.

To take care of certain rare hands, however, an immediate jump to four clubs by the responder over an opening bid of one or two no-trump is the Gerber Convention. Opener is required to bid:

Four diamonds to show *no* aces.

Four hearts to show *one* ace.

Four spades to show *two* aces.

Four no-trump to show *three* aces.

Five clubs to show *four* aces.

Sequence 35

OPENER	RESPONDER	OPENER	RESPONDER
♠ Q x x	♠ A K J x x x x	1 N-T	4 ♣
♥ A J x x	♥ K Q x x	4 ♠	6 ♠
♦ A x x	♦ x	Pass	
♣ K Q J	♣ x		

Responder knows that there is a small slam if his partner has two aces, and a grand slam if his partner has three aces. It is only on such strong and freakish hands that the Gerber Convention should be used.

CHAPTER VIII

Higher Opening Bids in No-trump

The Opening Bid of Two No-trump

The opening bid of two no-trump is made with a hand that

    (a) counts $22\frac{1}{2}$ to $24\frac{1}{2}$ points; and

    (b) has 4-3-3-3 or 4-4-3-2 or 5-3-3-2 (conveivably 6-3-2-2) distribution; and

    (c) has a stopper (Q-x-x, K-x, or better) in each of the four suits.

It will be seen that the range is quite narrow; just the value of a queen separates the weakest from the strongest possible opening bid of two no-trump. This makes it easy for responder to judge the value of his hand.

The reader may wonder what he should bid with hands that are slightly weaker or slightly stronger. For hands that count 20 to 22 points, see page 122–3. For hands that count 25 to $26\frac{1}{2}$ see page 109–110.

Suppose you have $22\frac{1}{2}$ to $24\frac{1}{2}$ points, but the wrong type of distribution. Bid one of a suit. With very unbalanced distribution, you might even open with a forcing two-bid. That is another story, however. The chief point now is that you do not open such hands with two no-trump.

What should you bid with the right count and the

right distribution but with one suit unstopped? Bid one of a suit. An opening bid of two no-trump guarantees a stopper in each of the four suits.

110. ♠ A Q x x ♥ A Q 10 x ♦ K J x ♣ A 10

Bid two no-trump. The count is 22½ points, a minimum opening bid of two no-trump. Don't worry about the two four-card major suits. Your partner will look for a fit if he has length in a major.

111. ♠ Q 10 x x ♥ K Q J ♦ A Q J ♣ A Q J

Bid two no-trump. The count is 23½ points, the middle value for an opening bid of two no-trump.

112. ♠ Q x x ♥ A K Q ♦ A K 10 ♣ K J 10 x

Bid two no-trump. The count is 24 points, so you have a maximum opening bid of two no-trump.

113. ♠ A 10 x ♥ A J 10 ♦ A K Q x x ♣ Q J

Bid one diamond. You have no stopper in clubs and therefore cannot open with two no-trump.

114. ♠ K Q ♥ A 10 ♦ A Q x x x ♣ A Q 10 x

Bid one diamond. The distribution is poor for an opening bid in no-trump. You will probably have the chance to bid no-trump vigorously later on.

Responding to Two No-trump

With 4 points or more, you respond to an opening bid of two no-trump. With less, you pass (except with very good distribution) and hope for the best. If the opening bid is doubled (an extremely rare occurrence) responder may rescue in any five-card or longer suit—provided the hand is a real bust. With 4 or more points it would be ridiculous to rescue; you would redouble.

Assuming (as is reasonable and most common) that

there is no interference bidding, your responses should conform to the following pattern:

Three Spades, Hearts, or Diamonds: You have a weak hand or you are not sure which final contract is best —game in some suit or in no-trump. Slam seems out of the question.

Four of a Major: Your hand is suited only to this contract. Slam seems remote.

Three No-trump: 4 to 10 points, usually flat distribution.

Four No-trump: 4-3-3-3 distribution, with 10½ to 12 points. Opener adds points and acts according to the total in the combined hands.

Five No-trump: 4-3-3-3 distribution, with 12½ to 14 points. Opener must bid six in his best suit (since it may provide a 4-4 fit), and the final contract will be six (but not seven) in a suit or no-trump.

Three Clubs: The 'Stayman' Convention. Opener must show a major or indicate the size of the no-trump—just as though the opening bid had been *one* no-trump (except that all bids are one trick higher). Responder promises 4 or more points, and may be looking for a game or for a slam.

Note that opener must not count his ten-spots when he rebids to show whether he had a minimum or a maximum. This information can be important only for slam purposes, and ten-spots are not counted for slams.

In general, development of the bidding follows the principles described at length in the chapters on the opening bid of one no-trump. The opener's strength is indicated within 2 points by the opening bid. Responder may try to get a narrower definition of opener's strength; or he may describe his own hand and leave the decision to opener.

Sequence 36

OPENER	RESPONDER	OPENER	RESPONDER
♠ K 10 x	♠ Q x x x x	2 N-T	Pass
♥ A Q J	♥ x x x		
♦ A J x	♦ x x x		
♣ K Q J x	♣ x x		

You do not try to rescue an opening bid of two no-trump. The moment you make any bid, the partnership must expect to reach game. There isn't enough room to begin and complete a sign-off.

Sequence 37

OPENER	RESPONDER	OPENER	RESPONDER
♠ K 10 x	♠ Q x x	2 N-T	3 N-T
♥ A Q J	♥ x x x	Pass	
♦ A J x	♦ Q 10 x		
♣ K Q J x	♣ x x x x		

There is no guarantee that this game contract will be made, but the play for it is quite adequate. Responder might have up to 10 points and would still bid only three no-trump with this distribution.

Sequence 38

OPENER	RESPONDER	OPENER	RESPONDER
♠ A x	♠ K x x x x	2 N-T	3 ♠
♥ A K x	♥ Q x x x x	3 N-T	4 ♥
♦ K Q x x	♦ x	Pass	
♣ K Q J x	♣ x x		

Responder sees that slam is out of the question. He wants to play the hand at game in one of the major suits. He first suggests game in spades, and then in

105

hearts. Note that opener does not dream of going beyond game. He has already shown his strength, and it is up to responder to take strong action if slam is a likelihood.

Sequence 39

OPENER	RESPONDER	OPENER	RESPONDER
♠ K 10 x	♠ Q J x x x	2 N-T	3 ♠
♥ A Q J x	♥ x x	4 ♠	Pass
♦ K Q J	♦ x x x x		
♣ A Q 10	♣ x x		

Responder counts 4 points, including 1 point for length in spades. He suggests game in his suit, and opener raises. Note that opener does not go beyond game even though he has a good fit for spades. Opener could make a mild slam try by bidding four clubs or four diamonds, if he had a maximum. Failure to bid three no-trump would guarantee ability to bid four spades.

Sequence 40

OPENER	RESPONDER	OPENER	RESPONDER
♠ K Q x	♠ J 10 x x	2 N-T	3 ♣
♥ K Q x	♥ J x x x	3 ♦	3 N-T
♦ K Q x	♦ x x x	Pass	
♣ A K x x	♣ Q x		

Responder uses the 'Stayman' Convention, trying to find a major suit fit. Opener bids three diamonds to show a minimum with no biddable major. Responder then proceeds to game in no-trump.

Sequence 41

OPENER	RESPONDER	OPENER	RESPONDER
♠ K Q x	♠ J 10 x x	2 N-T	3 ♣
♥ K Q x x	♥ J x x x	3 ♥	4 ♥
♦ A J x	♦ K x x	Pass	
♣ A K x	♣ x x		

Responder tries for a fit in a major suit, and the fit is discovered. Opener doesn't consider going past game because responder has shown no slam interest.

Sequence 42

OPENER	RESPONDER	OPENER	RESPONDER
♠ K 10	♠ Q J x x x	2 N-T	3 ♣
♥ A Q J x	♥ x x	3 ♥	3 ♠
♦ K Q J	♦ A 10 x x x	3 N-T	Pass
♣ K Q J x	♣ x		

As before, responder tries to find a major-suit fit. Opener shows biddable hearts, thus denying biddable spades. (As usual, he would show the higher suit first if he had both.) Responder bids the spades anyway, thus showing a five-card suit. Opener would raise spades with Q-x-x or better; otherwise, he bids three no-trump.

Sequence 43

OPENER	RESPONDER	OPENER	RESPONDER
♠ K Q x x	♠ J	2 N-T	3 ♣
♥ A Q J x	♥ K x x	3 ♠	3 N-T
♦ A x	♦ x x x x	4 ♥	Pass
♣ A K x	♣ J x x x		

Opener has biddable holdings in both major suits. When responder shows no enthusiasm for spades, opener shows the hearts.

There is no danger in disturbing three no-trump because responder would not bid three clubs unless he were ready for a ten-trick contract.

Sequence 44

OPENER	RESPONDER	OPENER	RESPONDER
♠ K Q	♠ J 10 x x x x x	2 N-T	3 ♠
♥ K Q x	♥ x x	3 N-T	4 ♠
♦ K Q x x	♦ x	Pass	
♣ A K x x	♣ x x x		

Responder wants to play the hand at game in spades and has good reason to believe that slam is out of the question. There should be a good play for game at spades, but even two no-trump might be in danger.

Sequence 45

OPENER	RESPONDER	OPENER	RESPONDER
♠ Q x x	♠ K J 10 x x x	2 N-T	3 ♣
♥ A Q J x	♥ K x x	3 ♥	4 ♠
♦ K Q J	♦ x	Pass	
♣ A K x	♣ x x x		

Responder, with 9 points and a singleton, can see that a slam is possible. He makes a mild slam try by jumping to four spades when three spades would be forcing.

Opener, with a minimum, cannot accept the mild invitation. If opener had a maximum he might go on.

Sequence 46

OPENER	RESPONDER	OPENER	RESPONDER
♠ A 10 x	♠ K x x x	2 N-T	3 ♣
♥ K Q 10	♥ A x	3 ♦	3 N-T
♦ K J x	♦ Q 10 x	Pass	
♣ A K Q x	♣ J x x x		

Opener shows a minimum ($22\frac{1}{2}$ to $23\frac{1}{2}$ points) without a biddable major. Responder, with $10\frac{1}{2}$ points (not counting the ten) would try for a slam if opener had shown a maximum. Since opener shows a minimum, responder bids only game.

Note that opener has only 23 points when he ignores his ten-spots.

Sequence 47

Opener	Responder	Opener	Responder
♠ K Q x	♠ 10 x x x	2 N-T	3 ♣
♥ K Q x x	♥ A J x x	3 ♥	4 ♣
♦ A K J	♦ x x	5 ♣	6 ♥
♣ A J 10	♣ K Q x	Pass	

Responder, with $10\frac{1}{2}$ points, can see a slam if opener has a maximum and a fit. He bids four clubs to mark time and get a reaction. When opener bids five clubs, responder is encouraged enough to bid the slam in hearts. With a minimum, opener would avoid getting to the level of five.

Sequence 48

Opener	Responder	Opener	Responder
♠ A Q x x	♠ K x x	2 N-T	3 ♣
♥ K 10	♥ Q x x	3 ♠	5 N-T
♦ K 10 x x	♦ A Q J x	6 ♦	Pass
♣ A K Q	♣ 10 x x		

Responder, with $12\frac{1}{2}$ points, is willing to reach slam opposite any kind of two no-trump bid. His jump to five no-trump tells opener to bid six but not seven; and denies strong spade support, since responder would bid six spades himself if he could. Opener can afford to bid six diamonds on the way to six no-trump. Responder happens to fit, so passes.

The Opening Bid of Two Clubs

The opening bid of two clubs is forcing and artificial. Opener may have:

(a) *A no-trump hand* that counts to more than $24\frac{1}{2}$ points, or

(b) *A suit hand* that is worth some eventual game contract.

The opener may or may not have biddable clubs. His partner must respond at least once, and the opener will then clarify the situation.

Since the rebid depends on the response, let us first see what the responder is permitted to do.

Responses to Two Clubs

The responder may make a positive response only if he has:

1. At least an ace and a king; or three kings; or K-Q in one suit and a side king; or

2. A five-card (or longer) suit headed by at least K-Q or A-J.

In case 1, responder shows any biddable suit. Lacking a biddable suit, he may bid two no-trump (positive response) with a count of $7\frac{1}{2}$ to $8\frac{1}{2}$ points; or three no-trump with a count of 9 to 10 points. With more than 10 points responder should manufacture a suit response whether or not he has a biddable suit. (But responder must make the negative response regardless of his count if he lacks the specific high cards listed in case 1 above.)

In case 2, responder bids the long suit.

Note that there is no such thing as 'raising' to three clubs. Opener does not promise a club suit, and responder bids three clubs only if he is willing to show clubs as his own suit.

If responder cannot make a positive response, he bids two diamonds—the negative response. Responder may bid two diamonds with several queens and jacks and even a king or so; but, in that case, responder will make at least one vigorous bid later on.

The positive response in diamonds must be *three* diamonds, since two diamonds is reserved for the negative response.

Opener's Rebids in No-trump

When the opener's first rebid is in no-trump, he shows that he has a no-trump type of hand[1] that counts to more than $24\frac{1}{2}$ points.

The opener may have:

1. *A big two no-trump hand* (25 to $26\frac{1}{2}$ points). He will open with two clubs and make a minimum rebid in no-trump at his next turn.

2. *A game-going no-trump hand* (27 to $28\frac{1}{2}$ points). He will open with two clubs and make a jump rebid in no-trump at his next turn.

It will be seen that the opener has the range of $22\frac{1}{2}$ to $26\frac{1}{2}$ points for bids of two no-trump. With $22\frac{1}{2}$ to $24\frac{1}{2}$, he simply bids two no-trump. With 25 to $26\frac{1}{2}$, he bids two clubs and then makes a minimum rebid in no-trump at his next turn.

This device enables the responder to bid intelligently when he has only 3 points (only a king, or a queen and a jack, in the entire hand). He can safely pass an opening bid of two no-trump; very few games will be missed. He can safely respond to an opener who bids two clubs

[1] His first rebid shows his best suit if he has the suit type of hand. The idea of opening with two clubs and rebidding in no-trump to show a very strong no-trump hand was borrowed from the Acol System. I have, however, assigned different values to these no-trump bids and have combined them with the 'Stayman' Convention to make it easy to find a suit fit.

and then two no-trump. This is the answer to the problem discussed on page 20.

The opener's rebid of two no-trump (when he has begun with two clubs) is not forcing. Responder may pass with less than 2 points. With 2 points or more, responder carries on to game.

If responder's first bid is three clubs or three diamonds, opener must bid three no-trump with his big two no-trump hand, and four no-trump with his game-going no-trump hand. Both bids are quite safe since responder has at least 7½ points.

If responder's first bid is two no-trump or three no-trump, opener can add points and proceed according to the combined total.

The 'Stayman' Convention is used in the following bidding situations:

OPENER	RESPONDER		OPENER	RESPONDER
2 ♣	2 ♦		2 ♣	2 ♦
2 N-T	3 ♣		3 N-T	4 ♣

Responder's bid of three clubs or four clubs asks the opener to show a biddable suit. With two biddable suits, opener bids the higher ranking. There is no distinction between major and minor suit at this level, nor does opener attempt to show whether he has a maximum or a minimum.

Sequence 49

OPENER	RESPONDER		OPENER	RESPONDER
♠ A Q x	♠ x x x		2 ♣	2 ♦
♥ A Q 10	♥ J x x		2 N-T	Pass
♦ A J 10 x	♦ x x			
♣ K Q J	♣ x x x x x			

Opener has the hand mentioned on page 20. Responder has a blank hand, and the auction dies at two no-trump. If responder had another jack he would raise to three no-trump. The play for game would be a bit sketchy, but not hopeless.

Sequence 50

Opener	Responder	Opener	Responder
♠ K Q x	♠ 10 x x x	2 ♣	2 ♦
♥ A K Q x x	♥ x	2 N-T	3 ♣
♦ A Q	♦ x x x x	3 ♥	3 N-T
♣ K x x	♣ Q x x x	Pass	

Opener counts 25 points including 1 point for length in hearts. The hand is not quite good enough for the suit-type of two-club bid, but it is well described by two clubs followed by two no-trump. Responder, with 2½ points, carries on. He bids the conventional three clubs, looking for a fit. When opener fails to bid spades, responder subsides at three no-trump.

Sequence 51

Opener	Responder	Opener	Responder
♠ K Q x	♠ x x x x x	2 ♣	2 ♦
♥ A K Q x	♥ x x x	2 N-T	3 ♠
♦ A Q x	♦ x x x	4 ♠	Pass
♣ K Q x	♣ x x		

Opener shows a big no-trump hand, and responder might pass since his hand is practically worthless. However, any five-card major suit should be bid. The chances are that four spades is as good a contract as two no-trump.

Sequence 52

Opener	Responder	Opener	Responder
♠ A J x	♠ K x x x	2 ♣	2 ♦
♥ K J x	♥ Q x x x	2 N-T	3 ♣
♦ A K x x	♦ x x x	3 ♦	3 N-T
♣ A K Q	♣ x x	Pass	

Opener shows a big two no-trump hand, and responder uses the 'Stayman' Convention. Opener is required to show his highest biddable suit (or bid three no-trump if his suit is clubs). In this situation, there is no need to show minimum or maximum since the range is so small. Opener shows his suit in the example. Responder goes to game in no-trump since no major suit fit has been found.

Sequence 53

OPENER	RESPONDER	OPENER	RESPONDER
♠ A J x	♠ K Q 10 x x	2 ♣	2 ♠
♥ A Q x x	♥ x x	2 N-T	3 N-T
♦ A Q J	♦ x x x	Pass	
♣ K Q 10	♣ x x x		

Responder makes a positive response, and opener then shows that his hand is a big two no-trump. If responder had enough values to try for a slam he would bid a new suit or jump in no-trump.

Sequence 54

OPENER	RESPONDER	OPENER	RESPONDER
♠ A K J x	♠ x x	2 ♣	2 ♥
♥ A J x	♥ K Q x x x	2 N-T	4 N-T
♦ A Q x	♦ K x x	6 N-T	Pass
♣ K Q J	♣ x x x		

Responder makes a positive response, and opener shows a big two no-trump. Responder invites a slam; and opener, with an absolute maximum and a fit for responder's suit, bids the slam at once.

Sequence 55

OPENER	RESPONDER	OPENER	RESPONDER
♠ A K x	♠ x x x	2 ♣	2 ♦
A K x	♥ Q x x	3 N-T	Pass
A K x x	♦ x x x		
K J 10	♣ x x x x		

Opener shows the enormous no-trump hand that can be satisfied with nothing less than game. Opener may not make three no-trump if responder has a completely blank hand with not even a minor fit somewhere. However, no good player can fail to bid game with such hands.

Sequence 56

OPENER	RESPONDER	OPENER	RESPONDER
A Q x x	♠ J 10 x x	2 ♣	2 ♦
A K J	♥ x x x x x	3 N-T	4 ♣
A Q x	♦ x x x x	4 ♠	Pass
K Q 10	♣ —		

Opener shows a game-going no-trump hand, and responder uses the 'Stayman' Convention to look for a fit. Opener does not distinguish between major and minor or between maximum and minimum. He just bids his highest biddable suit (or four no-trump if his only biddable suit is clubs). Responder is satisfied with four spades, so he passes.

Sequence 57

OPENER	RESPONDER	OPENER	RESPONDER
♠ A J x	♠ K Q 10 x x	2 ♣	2 ♠
A K 10 x	♥ x x	3 N-T	4 N-T
A Q J	♦ x x x	6 N-T	Pass
A Q J	♣ x x x		

When opener shows the biggest kind of no-trump hand, responder sees a chance for slam. (Compare with

Sequence 53, in which responder is satisfied with game.)
Responder may invite a slam by making any bid in
this case—even four spades. There would be no need
to disturb three no-trump if only game were being considered. Opener gladly accepts the invitation.

Sequence 58

OPENER	RESPONDER	OPENER	RESPONDER
♠ A J x x	♠ K Q x	2 ♣	3 ♣
♥ A K x	♥ x x x	4 N-T	5 N-T
♦ A K J	♦ x x	6 N-T	Pass
♣ A Q x	♣ K x x x x		

Opener must jump to four no-trump to show the full
value of the hand. (A bid of only three no-trump would
indicate only 25 to 26½ points.) Responder's bid of five
no-trump tells opener to choose his small slam.)

Sequence 59

OPENER	RESPONDER	OPENER	RESPONDER
♠ A Q x	♠ K x x	2 ♣	3 N-T
♥ A Q J	♥ K x x	6 N-T	Pass
♦ A Q x x	♦ K x x		
♣ K Q J	♣ x x x x		

Opener had planned to make a minimum rebid in
no-trump, but changes his mind when responder shows
9 to 10 points without a biddable suit. Opener adds
points and finds that the total must be 35½ to 36½ points.
He therefore bids the slam at once. The slam would be
lay-down if opener had the jack of diamonds instead of
the jack of hearts or if responder had the jack of diamonds. Even as it is, the play is adequate.

The Opening Bid of Three No-trump

Most American players use the opening bid of three no-trump to show a balanced hand of enormous power. Some few use the opening bid of three no-trump to show a hand with a long solid suit and a gambling chance to get in and run that suit.

Whichever of these courses a player adopts, there are times when he wishes he had done the opposite. He can't alter the meaning of the bid according to the type of hand he gets because his partner would never know when to act and when to pass discreetly.

The problem is solved very easily in this system. The enormous no-trump hand is opened with two clubs, followed by a jump in no-trump. This leaves the opening bid of three no-trump for the gambling type of hand.

115. ♠ K x ♥ K x ♦ A K Q x x x x ♣ Q x

Bid three no-trump. You have a good chance to win eight tricks quickly if a major suit is led. Sometimes you will make nine tricks when the opponents had game-going values against you.

116. ♠ K x ♥ J x x ♦ A K Q J x x ♣ K x

Bid three no-trump. This type of bid is especially useful after two passes. It gives you a chance at game and acts as a shut-out bid at the same time.

117. ♠ x x x ♥ x ♦ x x ♣ A K Q x x x x

Bid three no-trump after two passes if not vulnerable against vulnerable opponents. This is in the nature of a psychic bid and is a better pre-empt than three clubs. You might even make three no-trump against opponents who could make a game in some suit.

Running Out

Your first thought about such gambling bids may be that you must run to the safety of your suit if an opponent doubles. This is not such a good idea as it may seem to be.

If you make it your standard practice to run out, clever opponents will double with any excuse. Why should they let you play for a game when they can drive you to four of a minor?

Moreover you are not always better off at four of your suit than at three no-trump. You will feel very foolish if you go down one at your suit when you could have made three no-trump.

CHAPTER IX

Other Bids in No-trump

We have already discussed all opening bids in no-trump. There remain to be considered no-trump rebids, responses, and overcalls. All such bids show no-trump distribution together with a definite and narrowly limited range of strength.

Overcall of One No-trump

The overcall of one no-trump shows:

(a) $17\frac{1}{2}$ to 20 points (exactly the same as an opening bid of one no-trump).

(b) No-trump distribution: 4-3-3-3, 4-4-3-2, or 5-3-3-2 (conceivably 6-3-2-2).

(c) A stopper in each suit bid by the opponents.

As a general rule, a take-out double is preferred on a strong hand that includes good four-card support for the unbid major suit. Hence when a no-trump overcall is made over a major suit, the inference may be drawn that the no-trump hand does not contain strong four-card support for the other major suit.

If the no-trump overcall is made when no major suit has been bid, the no-trump hand may include good four-card support for one major suit but is unlikely to include such support for both majors.

In any case, however, a response of two clubs to the no-trump overcall is the 'Stayman' convention. Responses and rebids have the same meaning that they would have if the no-trump overcall had been an opening bid.

Opener's Rebid of One No-trump

The bidding has proceeded:

SOUTH	WEST	NORTH	EAST
1 ♦	Pass	1 ♥	Pass
1 N-T			

What is shown by the rebid of one no-trump?

Opener shows mainly that he cannot do anything better. One no-trump is a weak rebid.

(a) He cannot rebid his suit. His suit may be too weak for a rebid. Sometimes his suit is technically rebiddable, but the hand is such a minimum that the weak no-trump rebid best describes the hand.

(b) He cannot raise responder's suit. He may have one, two or three cards in responder's suit but rarely four-card support.

(c) He cannot bid a new suit. He does not have another biddable suit to show. (In some bidding situations, opener cannot show a new suit without making a 'reverse' bid. A rebid of one no-trump in such a case does not definitely deny a biddable holding in one of the unbid suits.)

(d) *He does not have more than* 16 *points.* With 16½ points or more, he must manufacture some other rebid—a new suit (even if theoretically unbiddable), a raise, or a rebid of his own suit.

Responder can afford to pass any balanced hand of 11 points or less, since the total should not produce a game.

The bidding has proceeded:

SOUTH	WEST	NORTH	EAST
1 ♦	Pass	1 ♥	Pass
?			

118. ♠ Q x x ♥ x x ♦ A J x x x ♣ A K x

Bid one no-trump. This is a maximum holding for the weak rebid of one no-trump.

119. ♠ Q x x ♥ x x ♦ A J 10 x x ♣ A K x

Bid two diamonds. Your hand counts 15½ for high cards and probably one point for length in diamonds. The rebid of two diamonds is not necessarily stronger than a rebid of one no-trump; but a rebid of one no-trump is definitely weak, while a rebid of two diamonds can show slightly greater strength. To put it another way, the two rebids have the same floor, but different cielings.

120. ♠ Q x x ♥ 10 x ♦ A Q x x x ♣ A K x

Bid two clubs. Your count is 16½ points plus the value of your length in diamonds. A conservative player might rebid diamonds, but a rebid of two clubs is more informative. If partner has to pass, you will not miss a game, and the chances are that two clubs will not be far inferior to two diamonds.

The bidding has proceeded:

SOUTH	WEST	NORTH	EAST
1 ♣	Pass	1 ♠	Pass
1 N-T	Pass	?	

121. ♠ A Q x x ♥ K x x x ♦ J x ♣ 10 x x

Pass. This is a balanced hand counting to exactly 11 points (an average hand). Opener has a maximum of 16 points, so that the combined total is 27 points at best. It is unlikely that you will have a good play for game.

122. ♠ A x x x ♥ x x x ♦ A Q x ♣ x x x

Pass. Your high card strength looks impressive, but the total is only 11 points. There is unlikely to be any sound play for game.

123. ♠ K Q J x x ♥ K x x ♦ Q x ♣ x x x

Bid two spades. Your hand counts 11 points in high cards and the spade length is surely worth at least one point. There may very well be a play for game if the opener has close to his maximum of 16 points. If he has, he will bid again; if he has not, it would be foolish for you to make a jump bid and force to a game that is unlikely to make.

Opener's Jump Rebids in No-trump

The bidding has proceeded:

Sequence A		Sequence B	
OPENER	RESPONDER	OPENER	RESPONDER
1 ♥	1 ♠	1 ♥	2 ♣
2 N-T		3 N-T	

Sequence C	
OPENER	RESPONDER
1 ♥	1 ♠
3 N-T	

In Sequence A and Sequence B, opener shows:

(a) 20-22 points.

(b) No-trump distribution.

(c) A stopper in each of the unbid suits.

This may be the sort of hand that was too strong for one no-trump but not strong enough for two no-trump. Or it may be a 20-point hand with a weak doubleton in responder's suit.

In Sequence C, opener shows:

(a) 22 to 24½ points.

(b) No-trump distribution.

(c) A stopper in each of the unbid suits.

This is the sort of hand that was good enough for an opening bid of two no-trump, except that it did not contain a stopper in responder's suit or, conceivably, because the distribution was 5-4-2-2.

The bidding has proceeded:

OPENER	RESPONDER
1 ♥	1 ♠
?	

124. ♠ x x ♥ A K Q x ♦ A J 10 x ♣ K Q x

Bid two no-trump. Your count is 20½ points, and this jump rebid describes your hand much better than a rebid in diamonds.

125. ♠ A x x ♥ A K J x ♦ Q x x x ♣ A Q

Bid two no-trump. With 21½ points your hand was too strong for one no-trump but not strong enough for two no-trump. You show the nature of the hand by this jump rebid in no-trump. If partner's response had been two clubs, the proper rebid for the opener with this hand would be three no-trump.

126. ♠ x x ♥ A Q J x ♦ K 10 9 x ♣ A K 10

Bid two diamonds. Your count is only 19 points and you therefore cannot afford to jump to two no-trump.

127. ♠ J x ♥ A K J 10 ♦ A K x ♣ A J x x

Bid three no-trump. With a count of 23 points you want to make sure of getting to game once partner has responded. Since your hand is balanced and contains no long major suit, you bid the game in no-trump.

128. ♠ x x ♥ A K J 10 x ♦ A K ♣ A Q x x

Bid three clubs. As before, you have 23 points. In this case, however, game in a suit is a stronger possibility. If responder's next bid is three no-trump, you are perfectly willing to pass.

Jump Responses in No-trump

The bidding has proceeded:

Sequence A		Sequence B	
OPENER	RESPONDER	OPENER	RESPONDER
1 ♥	2 N-T	1 ♥	3 N-T

In Sequence A, responder shows:

(a) 14½ to 17 points.
(b) No-trump distribution.
(c) A stopper in each of the unbid suits.

In Sequence B, responder shows:

(a) 17½ to 18½ points (a minimum opening no-trump).
(b) No-trump distribution.
(c) A stopper in each of the unbid suits.

The bidding has proceeded:

OPENER	RESPONDER
1 ♥	?

124

129. ♠ K J 10 ♥ Q x x ♦ A Q x x ♣ Q J x

Bid two no-trump. With 16 points, balanced distribution, and a stopper in each of the unbid suits, you have an ideal response of two no-trump.

130. ♠ Q 10 x ♥ K x x ♦ A K x ♣ Q x x x

Bid two no-trump. This is a minimum, since you have only 15 points and since your stopper in each of the black suits is somewhat sketchy.

131. ♠ A J 10 ♥ x x ♦ K Q x x ♣ K Q J x

Bid two no-trump. This is a maximum, since you have 17 points and a very sound stopper in each of the unbid suits.

132. ♠ A 10 x ♥ K x x ♦ Q J x ♣ K Q J x

Bid two clubs (not two no-trump). With 17 points and a good fit for your partner's suit, you should avoid responding at two no-trump since you might very easily miss a slam.

133. ♠ K Q x ♥ J x ♦ Q J x x ♣ K Q x x

Bid two clubs. With a count of only 14 points your hand is not strong enough for a response of two no-trump.

134. ♠ A J x ♥ J x x ♦ K Q x ♣ A Q x x

Bid three no-trump. With a count of 18 points, balanced distribution, and strength in each of the unbid suits, you have an ideal jump to three no-trump.

135. ♠ A Q x ♥ J x x ♦ K Q x ♣ A Q x x

Bid three clubs. Since the hand counts 19 points, you are too strong to jump to three no-trump. If partner bids three no-trump, you will pass. If he makes a suit rebid, your next bid will be three no-trump. By this means, you can indicate that your hand is balanced in distribution but too strong for an immediate response of three no-trump.

Development of the Bidding

In all of the situations just described, one member of the partnership shows the point value of his hand by a jump bid in no-trump. The other member of the partnership can count his own points, compute the total in the combined hands, and thus know whether to stop at game, try for a slam, or simply *bid* a slam.

The important numbers to remember are:

Game: 27½ points (27 points if vulnerable).

Small Slam: 35 points (31 points if one hand has a singleton; 27 points if one hand is void of a suit—always provided there is little duplication of values).

Grand Slam: 39 points (somewhat less with unbalanced distribution, provided all four aces are held).

Sequence 60

DEALER	PARTNER	DEALER	PARTNER
♠ K Q J x x	♠ A x x	Pass	1 ♥
♥ 10 x	♥ A K J x	1 ♠	2 N-T
♦ K x x	♦ Q 10 9 x	?	
♣ J x x	♣ A Q		

This is the hand first described on page 14. Dealer knows that partner has a count of 20 to 22 points; and his own hand counts 11 points (including 1 point for spade length). The combined total cannot be more than 33 points—enough for a comfortable game, but insufficient for slam. Dealer should therefore bid three no-trump.

CHAPTER X

Forcing Opening Bids

Few experienced players will question the advisability of having some opening bid that is forcing to game. However, let us review the reasons for having such a bid in order to see how the need can best be answered.

1. *Reaching Game.* A forcing opening bid is needed to make sure that partner responds when he would pass a bid of one in a suit or even a bid of two no-trump. There are many hands that offer an adequate play for game opposite such very weak responding hands.

2. *Reaching Slam.* A forcing opening bid makes it easy to describe a hand that will make a slam opposite very slight values. Without the opening forcing bid, opener might often have to get past game to describe the full strength of his hand. With the opening forcing bid, it is almost always possible to stop at game when the play for slam is inadequate.

The Question of strength

There has been considerable disagreement as to the strength required for an opening forcing bid. In the early days of contract bridge, many players would make a forcing bid on any hand that contained about $5\frac{1}{2}$

honour tricks. This was not enough in the case of balanced hands without strong suits, and this practice was responsible for some very unsafe game contracts.

P. Hal Sims was the chief influence in the other direction. His followers required 'game in hand' for an opening forcing bid. Since such hands were almost never available, the bid didn't earn its keep.

In recent years most experts have come around to a compromise position. They force to game with a hand that will afford an *adequate* (not sure-fire) play for game if partner has some moderate kind of fit for a suit (e.g. three small cards in a particular suit; or perhaps a queen).

Responses

There is no such agreement on the best responses to an opening forcing bid. Some players insist that responder's first duty is to show his aces; others that responder should show his distribution.

If either side were overwhelmingly right, this controversy would have been settled years ago. The fact is, however, that there is great merit in both views.

If the opener has a very powerful suit, he doesn't want to hear about responder's distribution; he wants to know about specific aces and kings. If the opener has good support for one or two suits besides his own best suit, he wants to know about his partner's distribution.

It all depends on which type of hand the opener has. Current practice does not enable the opener to indicate which type of information he wants. As we will see, however, there is a very simple way to indicate the type of hand right at the opening bid.

Which Bid for Forcing?

In America, Howard Schenken was chiefly responsible for the revival of the two-club bid. Schenken wanted to use the two-bid as a mild shut-out, and he reserved two clubs as the forcing opening bid.

When two clubs is used as a game-forcing bid, the negative response is two diamonds rather than two no-trump. This gives the opener the chance to play the hand at no-trump if his hand is not too badly unbalanced. In cases where a very strong hand is partnered with a very weak hand, the defence is aided by exposure of the strong hand as dummy. The defenders seldom have this advantage against players who use two clubs as their forcing bid.

Experience has shown that there is no particular disadvantage in using two clubs as the sole game-forcing bid. This bid does not, however, solve the problem of responses.

Some time ago,[1] therefore, I suggested that the opening bid of two diamonds be reserved for the one-suit type of hand in which the opener wants to know about his partner's high cards. This left two clubs as a forcing opening bid that asked clearly for responder's distribution.

Both bids will be more fully described in separate sections. At this point it is necessary only to make a few general observations.

When a player opens with two clubs, he may be prepared to rebid in no-trump (see page 111). If his rebid is two no-trump, responder may pass with a count of less

---

[1] The idea came to me in England in May 1949, during a discussion with Peter Leventritt and Adam Meredith.

than 2 points. If opener's rebid is in a suit, he has a game-going hand of suit type. However, the opener will not insist on playing the hand at his own suit (since he has not opened with two diamonds); and he must be ready to show a second suit, to support responder's suit, or to play at no-trump.

The use of two clubs and two diamonds as the sole game-forcing opening frees the opening bid of two spades or two hearts for another purpose. My team-mates and I believe that these opening bids are best used as mild shut-outs (as described on page 152–3). As a matter of fact, not all of my team-mates have adopted the bid of two diamonds to show a one-suit hand. They prefer to use two diamonds as a weak bid (like two spades and two hearts); and other players may prefer to follow their example rather than mine.

The Opening Bid of Two Clubs

The opening bid of two clubs:

(a) Forces to game (unless the opener's first rebid is two no-trump—see page 111).

(b) Is artificial (does not promise a club suit).

(c) Offers some sort of choice. The opener will not absolutely insist in playing the hand at his own long suit.

We have already seen that strong balanced hands are best described by various no-trump bids or by no-trump rebids. We have also seen that the very strongest no-trump hands are best described by an opening bid of two clubs and a no-trump rebid. What sort of hand, however, is described by an opening bid of two clubs and a suit rebid?

Distribution: Usually the pattern will be unbalanced: 5-4-3-1, 5-5-2-1, 6-4-2-1, etc., and even 4-4-4-1. Occasionally, opener will have 5-3-3-2, with a very good suit. (Opener may have no-trump distribution with 29 points or more.)

Strength: When the hand is fairly balanced, it must contain enough high-card strength to afford an adequate play for game—about 27 points. As opener's distribution becomes more and more unbalanced, his point count may be reduced. For unbalanced hands, no definite count can be assigned, but opener can tell at a glance whether or not he wants to be in a game with a dummy that contains only a very modest kind of fit.

136. ♠ A Q x ♥ A x ♦ A K Q x x ♣ A K x

Bid two clubs. This hand counts 28 points, without counting length in diamonds. You will rebid in diamonds, but will then be willing to support either black suit or no-trump.

137. ♠ A K Q x x ♥ A Q x ♦ x ♣ A K x x

Bid two clubs. The count for high cards is only 23½ points, while 27½ points are usually needed for game. The unbalanced distribution should compensate for the missing points.

138. ♠ x ♥ A Q J x x ♦ A x ♣ A K J 10 x

Bid two clubs. The count for high cards is only 21 points, but this is enough with a really strong two-suiter. You are willing to play for game if partner has a few small hearts or clubs.

139. ♠ A K x x ♥ x ♦ A K x x ♣ A K J x

Bid two clubs. This is a borderline case, but it is impossible to describe adequately so strong a three-suiter except by a forcing opening bid. If you open with a one-bid, you will probably have to bid past game to show the full strength of the hand. It must be admitted that this hand may fail to produce a game, but you cannot always achieve full safety.

140. ♠ A K x ♥ A K x ♦ A K x ♣ A Q x x

Bid two clubs. With a count of 29 points, you want to coax your partner to bid any miserable five-card suit; and you will then make a slam try. If partner shows no suit, you are willing to get up to four no-trump. Not completely safe, but well worth the risk.

Responses to Two Clubs

Positive Responses: Bid two spades, two hearts, three diamonds, or three clubs with some sort of biddable suit and a hand that contains:

(a) an ace and a king; or
(b) king-queen in one suit and king in another; or
(c) any three kings.

These values may be reduced when the hand contains a good suit. Make a positive response in any five-card (or longer) suit headed by K-Q or A-J (or better) even if the hand is otherwise worthless.

If the hand contains no biddable suit, bid two no-trump (a positive response) to show a count of $7\frac{1}{2}$ to $8\frac{1}{2}$ points; bid three no-trump to show 9 to 10 points. With more than 10 points, manufacture a suit response in an unbiddable suit. Remember that when you make a positive response in no-trump you always have the guaranteed high cards (A, K; or K-Q, K; or K, K, K). Do not count ten-spots for the positive responses in no-trump. These bids are steps in the direction of a slam, and ten-spots are never counted in such bidding.

Negative Response: Bid two diamonds on any hand that does not qualify for a positive response. You may have a fairly good hand that lacks the guaranteed high cards, or you may have any lesser hand—down to a complete bust.

141. ♠ x x x x x ♥ A x ♦ K x ♣ x x x x

Bid two spades. Any five-card suit is worth a response if you have the guaranteed high cards.

142. ♠ A x x ♥ x x x ♦ x x x ♣ A x x x

Bid three clubs. This is a pretty poor suit, but opener does not rely on anything better unless you rebid. You avoid making a positive response in no-trump when you can find a way of giving specific information.

143. ♠ K x ♥ K x x ♦ K x x x ♣ x x x x

Bid three diamonds. The jump is necessary because two diamonds would be the negative response.

144. ♠ x x ♥ A Q J 10 x x ♦ A x ♣ x x x

Bid two hearts. Obviously, this hand will be bid to a slam, but there is no need to get excited at this point.

145. ♠ K Q x x x ♥ x x x ♦ x x ♣ x x x

Bid two spades. This is a minimum holding for a positive response. You will make minimum rebids later.

146. ♠ K Q x x x ♥ K x x ♦ A x x x ♣ x

Bid two spades. You will bid this hand vigorously later on. Your only questions are which suit will be trump and whether to bid six or seven in that suit.

147. ♠ 10 x x x ♥ K Q x ♦ K x x ♣ x x x

Bid two no-trump. You have a count of 8 points but have no biddable suit.

148. ♠ A x x ♥ K x x ♦ Q 10 x ♣ x x x x

Bid three no-trump. You have a count of 9½ points without a biddable suit. Note that you don't count the ten of diamonds.

149. ♠ x x x ♥ A J x ♦ A x x ♣ J x x x

Bid three clubs. Your count of 11 points makes your hand too good for a response of three no-trump. The clubs are not biddable but that will not matter since the opener will have a suit to show and you can support that.

150. ♠ K J x ♥ K x x ♦ Q x x ♣ Q J x x

Bid two diamonds. You will next jump to four no-trump, thus showing a hand with a high point count but lacking the particular high cards guaranteed by a positive response.

151. ♠ x x x ♥ x x x ♦ x x x ♣ x x x x

Bid two diamonds. The negative response is, of course, made with a completely worthless hand.

152. ♠ K J 10 x x x ♥ x x x ♦ x x ♣ x x

Bid two diamonds. You cannot make a positive response in spades since you do not have the guaranteed high cards.

Interference Bidding

When the bidding has been opened with two clubs, a clever opponent will sometimes make an interference bid. Responder should make his normal positive response when possible; may double for penalties without guaranteeing the high cards needed for a positive response; and may pass with a hand that is not worth a positive response. However, responder should not bid no-trump without a stopper in the opponent's suit.

The bidding has proceeded:

SOUTH	WEST	NORTH	EAST
2 ♣	2 ♥	?	—

153. ♠ x x   ♥ Q 10 x x x   ♦ x x x   ♣ x x x

Double. This indicates only that you expect to defeat the doubled contract. Your double does not guarantee any high cards.

154. ♠ K x x x   ♥ x x   ♦ K x x   ♣ K x x x

Bid two spades. This would have been your response if there had been no interference bid. There is no reason to suppress this natural positive response.

155. ♠ K Q x   ♥ K x   ♦ x x x x   ♣ x x x x

Bid two no-trump. You have the normal point count guaranteed by this positive response; you have the guaranteed high cards; and you have a stopper in the enemy's suit.

156. ♠ x x x x   ♥ x x x   ♦ K x x   ♣ A x x

Pass. You have the values for a positive response but cannot afford to bid two no-trump without a stopper in the enemy's suit. You can afford to pass at this point and bid strongly later on.

Development of the Bidding

As in all systems, there is an exchange of information after the opening bid and first response. This is indicated in the examples that follow.

Sequence 61

OPENER	RESPONDER	OPENER	RESPONDER
♠ x	♠ K J 10 x x x x	2 ♣	2 ♦
♥ A K Q x x	♥ x	2 ♥	2 ♠
♦ A Q J x x	♦ x x x	3 ♦	4 ♠
♣ A x	♣ x x	Pass	

Responder must first make the negative response. Opener shows his strong hearts, and responder can mention spades. Opener then asks for a choice between the red suits, but responder can insist on spades. If opener's spades and clubs were exchanged, he would consider a slam; but with his actual cards, he must pass.

Sequence 62

OPENER	RESPONDER	OPENER	RESPONDER
♠ A x x	♠ K x x	2 ♣	2 ♦
♥ A K Q x x	♥ x x	2 ♥	2 N-T
♦ x	♦ J x x x x	3 ♣	3 ♦
♣ A K J x	♣ x x x	3 ♥	3 N-T
		Pass	

Responder makes the negative response, and opener then shows his strong suit. The partnership winds up in no-trump, since no sound suit contract is available.

Sequence 63

OPENER	RESPONDER	OPENER	RESPONDER
♠ A Q J x x	♠ K x x	2 ♣	2 ♥
♥ —	♥ A J x x	2 ♠	3 ♠
♦ K Q J x x	♦ x x x x	4 ♦	4 ♠
♣ K Q x	♣ x x	Pass	

Responder can begin with a positive response in hearts and can then raise spades. Opener, however, cannot work up any enthusiasm over the heart response and therefore passes at game. Responder, with additional strength, would not have bid four spades.

Sequence 64

OPENER	RESPONDER	OPENER	RESPONDER
♠ x	♠ K x x x x	2 ♣	2 ♠
♥ A x x	♥ K Q J x x	3 ♣	3 ♥
♦ A Q J x	♦ x x	4 ♦	4 ♥
♣ A K Q x x	♣ x	5 ♥	6 ♥
		Pass	

Responder makes his first positive response in spades, the higher of his two suits. Opener bids clubs first and then diamonds, indicating the difference in length. When responder rebids the hearts, opener can afford to make a slam try. Responder naturally accepts.

The Opening Bid of Two Diamonds

The opening bid of two diamonds is artificial and forcing to game. The bid shows:

(a) A suit that is quite playable opposite a singleton.

(b) A total of at least nine sure tricks. There is no point requirement.

(c) A one-suit hand—not a two-suiter. Opener will insist on playing the hand at game or more in his own suit (or at *three* no-trump).

The opener's first rebid shows his real suit. Thereafter, the responder is not allowed to pass unless the opener has bid:

(a) three no-trump; or

(b) game (or higher) in his real suit. When opener makes such a rebid, responder *must* pass. (However, if

137

opener *jumps* to five of a major, he is making a slam invitation.)

157. ♠ — ♥ A K Q J x x x ♦ A x x ♣ A x x

Bid two diamonds. (Your first rebid will be in hearts.) Your hearts are playable opposite a singleton (or even a void), and you can confidently expect to win seven hearts and your two aces.

158. ♠ — ♥ K J 10 ♦ A K Q ♣ A K Q J 10 x x

Bid two diamonds. (Your first rebid will be in clubs.) Your clubs are, of course, independent. You can expect to win at least eleven tricks.

159. ♠ K Q J 10 x x x ♥ A Q x x ♦ A ♣ A

Bid two diamonds. (Your first rebid will be in spades.) Your spades need no support, and you expect to win at least nine tricks.

Responses to Two Diamonds

The negative response at any time is the minimum bid in no-trump. This response is made whenever responder cannot pass and also cannot make a positive response. (Responder should be on the alert to pass a bid of three no-trump or of game or more in opener's real suit.)

Positive Responses: Responder's first duty is to show his aces. If he is still required to bid, he next shows his kings. If he is required to bid even more, he shows his queens.

Choice of high card: With more than one ace, bid the highest ace first; then the next highest; and so on.

Distinguishing aces from kings: Responder always shows his highest ace first, and the next highest ace next, and so on. Before showing one king, responder must make a negative response (in no-trump) unless the rank of the king clarifies the situation automatically. Consider the following sequences:

Sequence A			Sequence B	
OPENER	RESPONDER		OPENER	RESPONDER
2 ♦	2 ♠		2 ♦	2 ♥
3 ♣	3 ♥		3 ♣	3 ♠

Sequence C	
OPENER	RESPONDER
2 ♦	2 ♠
3 ♣	3 N-T
4 ♣	4 ♥

In Sequence A, responder shows first the ace of spades and then the ace of hearts.

In Sequence B, responder shows first the ace of hearts and then the king of spades. The second bid cannot show an ace because the ace of spades would be shown before the ace of hearts.

In Sequence C, responder shows first the ace of spades; then no more aces, then the king of hearts. Note that responder cannot show the king of hearts at his second turn, for a bid of three hearts would show the ace (as in Sequence A).

Jump Responses: If responder has no aces but has two kings, he makes a jump bid in the suit of the higher king. With three kings, responder jumps in no-trump. Either jump bid may be made after responder has shown all of his aces.

Sequence D			Sequence E	
OPENER	RESPONDER		OPENER	RESPONDER
2 ♦	3 ♥		2 ♦	3 N-T

Sequence F		Sequence G	
OPENER	RESPONDER	OPENER	RESPONDER
2 ♦	2 ♠	2 ♦	2 ♠
3 ♣	4 ♠	3 ♣	4 N-T

In Sequence D, responder shows no aces but the king of hearts and one lower king.

In Sequence E, responder shows no aces, but three kings.

In Sequence F, responder first shows the ace of spades. The second bid shows no further aces, but the king of spades and one lower king.

In Sequence G, responder first shows the ace of spades. The second response shows no further aces but three kings.

Now return to Sequence B. When responder bids three spades he shows no further aces and no king other than the king of spades. If he had more aces, he would show them before mentioning kings. If he had more than one king he would make a jump response.

A similar inference is drawn from Sequence C. When responder bids three no-trump, he shows that he has no more aces and also that he cannot have two or more kings. He may have one king, and he may have no kings at all. Moreover, if he has one king, it will not be the king of spades since then the second response would be three spades.

Such inferences are the soul of this convention. The negative information often outweighs the positive.

160.   ♠ A x x   ♥ x x x   ♦ x x x   ♣ A x x x

Bid two spades. Your first duty is to show the aces, and with more than one ace, you must show the higher ace first. At your next turn you will bid clubs.

161. ♠ x x x x x　♥ A x　♦ K x　♣ x x x x

Bid two hearts. At your next turn you will have to bid no-trump. If you get another chance, you will bid diamonds to show the king.

162. ♠ K x x　♥ x x　♦ A x x x　♣ x x x x

Bid three diamonds to show the ace. At your next turn you will bid spades to show the king. (Compare with the previous example.)

163. ♠ x x x x　♥ A K x　♦ x　♣ K x x x x

Bid two hearts. At your next turn you will make a jump bid in hearts to show the king of hearts and one lower king.

164. ♠ Q J x x x x　♥ —　♦ x x x x x　♣ x x

Bid two no-trump to show no aces. At your next turn you will bid three no-trump to show no kings.

165. ♠ x x　♥ x x　♦ K x x　♣ Q J x x x x

Bid two no-trump. At your next turn you will bid the minimum in diamonds to show the king. Your failure to jump will then indicate that you have no other king.

166. ♠ Q x x　♥ K x x　♦ K x x　♣ x x x x

Bid three hearts. This shows that you have no aces, but that you do have the king of hearts and one lower king.

167. ♠ K x x　♥ K x x　♦ K J x x x x　♣ x

Bid three no-trump. This shows no aces, but three kings.

Development of the Bidding

The opening bidder is complete captain of the hand. He knows exactly which aces and kings (or perhaps queens) are of use to him. He can keep getting information by failing to return to his real suit. Whenever he has heard all he wants to know, he bids game in his real suit; and responder must pass.

Opener must be very careful to bid his real suit at his first rebid. Otherwise, responder will never know when to pass.

Sequence 65

OPENER	RESPONDER	OPENER	RESPONDER
—	♠ K x x	2 ♦	2 N-T
A K Q J x x x	♥ x	3 ♥	3 ♠
A x x	♦ x x x x x	3 N-T	Pass
A x x	♣ x x x x		

Responder first shows no aces and at his next response shows the king of spades but no other king. (With more than one king, responder would have made a jump bid in spades or in no-trump.) Opener sees that no slam is possible and that even game in hearts may be in doubt. Game in no-trump, however, is a certainty since responder has the king of spades. Opener therefore bids three no-trump, and responder must pass.

Sequence 66

OPENER	RESPONDER	OPENER	RESPONDER
♠ —	♠ K x x	2 ♦	3 N-T
A K Q J x x x	♥ x x x	5 ♥	Pass
A x x	♦ K x x x		
A x x	♣ K x x		

Responder shows three kings, but no aces. Opener could bring matters to a halt by bidding four hearts. The actual bid of five hearts invites responder to go on with any further values. Since responder has no unshown values, he passes.

Sequence 67

Opener	Responder	Opener	Responder
♠ —	♠ K x x x	2 ♦	3 ♣
A K Q J x x x	♥ x	4 ♥	Pass
A x x	♦ K x x x		
A x x	♣ Q x x x		

Responder shows no aces, but the king of spades and one lower king. Opener cannot expect a slam opposite these high cards. He therefore bids four hearts, and responder must pass.

Sequence 68

Opener	Responder	Opener	Responder
♠ —	♠ K Q x	2 ♦	2 ♥
K J 10	♥ A Q x	3 ♣	3 ♠
A K Q	♦ x x x x x	4 ♣	4 ♠
A K Q J 10 x x	♣ x x	4 N-T	5 ♥
		7 ♣	Pass

Opener's first rebid shows his real suit, but thereafter every bid forces responder to keep going. Responder first shows the ace of hearts (but not the ace of spades). His second bid shows the king of spades, but no other kings. His third bid shows the queen of spades (it is not safe to make a jump bid to show more than one queen). When asked to keep going, responder then shows the queen of hearts.

Sequence 69

Opener	Responder	Opener	Responder
♠ K Q J 10 x x x	♠ —	2 ♦	3 ♥
A Q x x	♥ K x x	6 ♠	Pass
♦ A	♦ K x x x x x		
♣ A	♣ x x x		

Responder shows no aces, but the king of hearts and one lower king. This is all the opener needs to bid six spades.

Sequence 70

OPENER	RESPONDER	OPENER	RESPONDER
K Q J 10 x x x	♠ x x	2 ♦	4 ♦
A Q x x	♥ J 10 x x x	4 ♠	Pass
A	♦ K x x x		
A	♣ K x		

Responder shows no aces, but the king of diamonds and one lower king. Opener cannot be interested in this sort of information and therefore bids game in spades. If 'normal' bidding were used, responder might bid three hearts and the partnership might then reach a very doubtful slam in hearts. Responder could probably not get to his hand to take the heart finesse.

Sequence 71

OPENER	RESPONDER	OPENER	RESPONDER
A K Q J x x x	♠ x x	2 ♦	3 ♣
A Q x	♥ K	3 ♠	5 ♥
K x	♦ J 10 x x x x x	6 N-T	Pass
x	♣ A K x		

Responder's first bid shows the ace of clubs, but no other ace. His second bid shows the king of hearts and one lower king. Opener can identify all of responder's high cards and can therefore tell that six no-trump cannot be defeated. Six spades might conceivably be defeated by a diamond ruff.

Sequence 72

OPENER	RESPONDER	OPENER	RESPONDER
♠ K Q J 10 x x x x	♠ —	2 ♦	3 ♦
♥ —	♥ Q J 10 x x x x	3 ♠	3 N-T
♦ K Q x	♦ A x x	4 ♣	5 ♣
♣ A x	♣ K x x	6 ♠	

Responder's first bid shows the ace of diamonds. The response of three no-trump not only shows no further aces but also denies the kings of spades, hearts, and diamonds. (Responder could bid 4 spades, 4 hearts, or 4 diamonds to show a king.) Opener asks for more information (four spades would be the sign-off) in the hope that responder has the king of clubs. When responder shows that card, opener bids slam at once.

Sequence 73

OPENER	RESPONDER	OPENER	RESPONDER
♠ A K Q J 10 x x	♠ x x	2 ♦	2 ♥
♥ x x	♥ A K x x	2 ♠	3 ♣
♦ —	♦ x x x x	3 ♠	5 ♥
♣ Q J 10 9	♣ A K x	5 N-T	6 ♣
		7 ♠	Pass

Responder first shows his two aces and then jumps in hearts to show the king of hearts and one lower king. Opener's bid of five no-trump in this case asks responder to name the other king. When it turns out to be the king of clubs, opener can bid the grand slam. If it had been in diamonds, opener would have bid only six spades.

Sequence 74

OPENER	RESPONDER	OPENER	RESPONDER
♠ A K Q J 10 x x	♠ x x	2 ♦	2 ♥
♥ x x	♥ A K x x	2 ♠	3 ♦
♦ —	♦ A K x x	3 ♠	5 ♥
♣ Q J 10 9	♣ x x x	5 ♠	Pass

K

Responder shows his aces, and opener encourages him to continue in the hope that the ace of clubs will also be shown. When responder then jumps to show the king of hearts and a lower king, opener must sign off for fear of losing two clubs. A slam is missed if responder's lower king is in clubs. Not every slam can be reached.

Sequence 75

OPENER	RESPONDER	OPENER	RESPONDER
♠ A K Q J 10 x x	♠ x x	2 ♦	2 ♥
♥ x x	♥ A Q x x	2 ♠	3 ♣
♦ —	♦ K x x x	3 ♠	4 ♦
♣ Q J 10 9	♣ A x x	5 ♣	6 ♠

Responder shows his two aces, and opener asks him to tell more. Responder then shows the diamond king —but no other king. Opener is reluctant to bid slam and depend solely on the club finesse (although such a slam bid could not be criticized) so merely invites a slam. Responder accepts the invitation because of the unshown queen of hearts.

Interference Bidding

Shrewd opponents will bid, when they can, to interfere with the exchange of information. It should be noted that the same interference bids would probably be made even if the opener were using a different system and had therefore made a different opening bid.

Responder should remember that the opener may have little defensive strength but certainly has offensive strength amounting to a minimum of nine tricks. Hence responder should avoid doubling the opponents for penalties unless he has sure trump tricks.

When the interference bid is *non-jump*, responder should:

(a) Make his normal response, if possible.

(b) Double, if his normal response would have been exactly what the opponent has bid.

(c) Pass as a negative response.

(d) Bid two no-trump (if possible) to show no aces but two kings. (With lesser values, the pass is the best negative response.)

When the interference bid is a *jump-bid*, responder should bid entirely naturally:

(a) A double is for penalties, shows trump tricks, and denies substantial high-card strength in the other three suits.

(b) A suit bid shows a strong suit, good enough to show at the required level, in a hand that contains at least two high cards (aces and kings).

(c) A no-trump bid shows one or two sure tricks in the opponent's suit; with possibly some side strength. (Side strength is unlikely, however, since the two bidders probably hold most of the pack between them.)

(d) A pass shows inability to bid or double, and may even show a completely blank hand.

The bidding has proceeded:

SOUTH	WEST	NORTH	EAST
2 ♦	2 ♠	?	—

168.　♠ x x　♥ K　♦ J 10 x x x x x　♣ A K x

Bid three clubs. Your normal response is not affected by the intervening bid.

169. ♠ A x ♥ x x x ♦ x x x x ♣ x x x x

Double. If West had passed you would have bid two spades. This is not a business double.

170. ♠ x x ♥ A x x ♦ x x x x ♣ x x x x

Pass. You can no longer make the normal response of two hearts. Your one ace is not enough to get excited about, but perhaps you will bid it later.

171. ♠ x x ♥ A x x ♦ K x x x ♣ x x x x

Bid three hearts, showing your ace. (This does not show heart king and one lower king, because with two kings you would bid two no-trump.) With two high cards, you have reason to make a free bid.

172. ♠ x x ♥ K x x ♦ K x x x ♣ x x x x

Bid two no-trump. This shows no aces, but two kings. It does not indicate a stopper in the opponent's suit.

173. ♠ x x ♥ K x x ♦ K x x x ♣ K x x x

Bid three no-trump. This jump in no-trump is the normal response, showing three kings. It is not affected by the intervening bid. It does not necessarily indicate a stopper in the opponent's suit.

The bidding has proceeded:

SOUTH	WEST	NORTH	EAST
2 ♦	4 ♥	?	—

174. ♠ x x ♥ K ♦ J 10 x x x x x ♣ A K x

Bid five diamonds. This is a natural bid. The chances are that opener had solid spades and will go on in that suit. If he decides to stab at a slam, your hand should give him the required help.

175. ♠ x x ♥ Q 10 9 x x ♦ x x x ♣ x x x

Double. This is, of course, a penalty double. Even

though opener may contribute very little defensive strength, you should defeat four hearts. At any other contract you hand is probably worthless.

176. ♠ K x x ♥ x x x ♦ K Q x x ♣ x x x

Pass. Your hand does not qualify for any bid, but you intend to raise as soon as opener shows which black suit he holds. Your high cards should be helpful, and opener should be extremely short in hearts. This will be a stab, but it cannot be helped. We know that there is no sure defence against good pre-emptive bidding; one can but do one's best.

CHAPTER XI

Pre-emptive Bids

In a book written for experienced players there is no
need to explain at length the advantage of pre-emptive
bidding. We can summarize them and then proceed to
a discussion of how to turn them to account.

1. *Shut-Out:* Often your pre-emptive bid shuts the
opponents out of the auction. They will usually discover that they have missed some worthwhile objective
—a slam, a game, even a part score. Meanwhile, your
side makes a plus score of its own (sometimes as much as
a game) or sustains a trifling loss.

2. *Crowding and Confusion:* If the opponents refuse to
be shut out, they must find their best contract in very
few rounds of bidding. Some hands do not suffer from
this sort of treatment, but many do. If they find the
wrong contract and go down instead of scoring game,
their loss is about 600 points. You can afford a few small
losses on some pre-empts if others bring in profits of this
size.

3. *Pressure:* If you seldom pre-empt, the opponents
can play a relaxed game. If you make full use of pre-
empts, the opponents must modify their own bidding
methods to meet the threat. This will sometimes bring
you a profit on a hand where no pre-empt is actually

made, but where one opponent merely feared that a pre-empt *might* be made. This is hard to define, but is one aspect of the fact that some opponents are easier to play against than others—even when they appear to be equally skilful.

4. *Escaping a Double:* Players known to make sound pre-emptive bids seldom get doubled. When the strength is divided, neither opponent has enough to act; and even when it is concentrated in one hand, that opponent may decide to bid or may have trouble making a double that sticks. In short, the safest time to sacrifice is before, not after, the opponents have bid their game (or slam).

There is no sure defence against a good pre-emptive bid. It's hard enough to reach the best contract in some hands even when you can exchange information very 'scientifically' with your partner; but it's much harder when a pre-empt robs you of two or three levels of bidding.

Therefore your ideal bidding system is one that prepares for delicate, scientific bidding when your side has top control and that interferes with the opponents when *they* have top control. That interference is safe only when your side has a strong trump suit.

A strong trump suit is sometimes divided fairly evenly between you and your partner; but at other times one of you has exceptional length, while the other has only mild support. If you are going to make full use of pre-emptive bids, you must recognize both situations quickly and easily; and you must then act to throw up a barrage against the enemy.

Everybody is familiar with these principles in the case of opening bids of three and four (and five). Such a bid promises a long suit, and the pre-empt is accomplished by the opening bid.

Another familiar example is the case of a jump raise after a take-out double. For example:

SOUTH	WEST	NORTH	EAST
1 ♠	Double	3 ♠	—

North has enough spades to feel sure that a strong trump suit is available. He acts against the announced strength of the take-out double.

However, there are several other situations that should be treated in the same way. We will merely list them now and will discuss each under a separate heading.

1. Weak opening two-bids (see pages 152–3). This is the poor man's three-bid or four-bid.

2. Jump overcalls (see page 158). It's better to preempt after an opponent has bid than never to pre-empt at all.

3. Double raises when an opponent has entered the auction (see page 164). This extends the jump raise that follows a take-out double to all sorts of competitive bidding situations.

4. Double jump responses. This is a highly informative but also pre-emptive response to an opening bid or to a take-out double.

Weak Two-bids

The opening bid of two spades or two hearts suggests a game-forcing hand to most American players. Some years ago, however, Howard Schenken suggested using such bids as mild shut-outs. The suggestion was tried out in expert competition and was adjudged a great success.

An opening bid of two spades (or two hearts) following this method, shows:

1. A hand that does not qualify for an opening bid of one spade (or one heart); and

2. A good suit of five or more cards (usually six); and

3. A total of five to seven reasonably sure playing tricks (five playing tricks only when not vulnerable, seven only when vulnerable against non-vulnerable opponents); and

4. Usually, weakness in the other major suit. It is seldom either wise or necessary to pre-empt when you have both majors. This tendency may be relaxed if partner has already passed.

Responses to Weak Two-bids

A raise to three is invitational.

A raise to four (game) indicates that there is likely to be a play for game but that slam should be out of the question.

Any other response (except a penalty double) is forcing *on the opener* for one round. Responder may decide to drop at his next turn. If responder's second bid is merely three of opener's suit, opener may pass; responder will jump to game when he has the values. Hence responder may psych at his first response if he is ready to raise opener's suit.

Responder's action is based on knowledge of opener's type of hand. In general, he bids very much as though an opponent had opened and his partner had made an overcall at the level of two.

The general nature of the opening bid and of various responses is indicated in the examples that follow:

Sequence 76

OPENER	RESPONDER	OPENER	RESPONDER
♠ Q J 10 x x x	♠ A x x	2 ♠	3 ♠
♥ x	♥ K x x x	Pass	
♦ A x x x	♦ x x		
♣ x x	♣ A J x x		

Opener has about four playing tricks in spades and one in diamonds. His bid is sound if he is not vulnerable. Responder has the equivalent of a weak opening bid but knows that opener has less than an opening bid. Hence responder can invite a game but cannot bid it by himself. Opener would go on with six playing tricks, but passes with only five.

Sequence 77

OPENER	RESPONDER	OPENER	RESPONDER
♠ A J 10 x x x	♠ K x x	2 ♠	3 ♠
♥ x	♥ K x x x	4 ♠	Pass
♦ K x x x	♦ A Q x x		
♣ x x	♣ x x		

Opener has about 5½ playing tricks: about 4½ in spades and 1 in diamonds. Responder, as in Sequence 76, raises on the equivalent of a weak opening bid. This time opener accepts the invitation, although a pass could not be criticized.

Sequence 78

OPENER	RESPONDER	OPENER	RESPONDER
♠ K Q 10 x x x	♠ J x x x	2 ♠	4 ♠
♥ x x	♥ A K x x x	Pass	
♦ K x	♦ x x		
♣ x x x	♣ A x		

Opener should reserve this skimpy sort of hand for times when he is non-vulnerable against vulnerable opponents. If a two-bid is made on really bad hands, responder has no idea when to proceed, and the oppoents may profitably double. In this case, responder should jump to game since a raise to three can be passed.

Sequence 79

OPENER	RESPONDER	OPENER	RESPONDER
♠ x x	♠ A Q J x x	2 ♥	2 ♠
♥ A K J 10 x x	♥ x x	3 ♥	Pass
♦ x x	♦ A x		
♣ x x x	♣ J x x x		

Opener has 5 or 6 playing tricks. Responder can afford one constructive bid since he has a good hand. (His bid is not a rescue of opener; a two-bid is practically never rescued.) Opener has poor distribution and not quite 6 playing tricks so rebids only three hearts. Compare with Sequence 80.

Sequence 80

OPENER	RESPONDER	OPENER	RESPONDER
♠ x	♠ A x x	2 ♥	3 ♦
♥ K Q J 10 x x	♥ x x	4 ♥	Pass
♦ x x	♦ A K Q x x		
♣ K x x x	♣ x x x		

Opener has 6 playing tricks and good distribution. When responder makes a constructive bid, opener should jump to game. If opener rebid only three hearts, responder would probably pass. Compare with Sequence 79.

Sequence 81

Opener	Responder	Opener	Responder
♠ x	♠ Q x x	2 ♥	2 N-T
♥ K J 10 x x x	♥ x x	3 ♥	Pass
♦ K x	♦ A Q x x		
♣ 10 x x x	♣ A J x x		

Opener has an even skimpier hand than in Sequence 78, but his distribution is better. Responder suggests game, but opener must show his weakness by a minimum rebid in his suit. Responder would continue if he had a really powerful hand, but in this case he must pass.

Sequence 82

Opener	Responder	Opener	Responder
♠ x	♠ K x x x	2 ♥	2 N-T
♥ A Q J x x x	♥ K x	3 ♣	4 ♥
♦ x x x	♦ A Q x	Pass	
♣ K J x	♣ Q x x x		

Responder suggests a game by bidding two no-trump. Opener shows willingness to bid game by any rebid other than the minimum in his long suit.

If responder had been fooling, he would go back to three hearts, and opener would discreetly pass. Since responder has the merchandise and knows that opener has more than a minimum, he jumps to game.

Sequence 83

Opener	Responder	Opener	Responder
♠ K Q 10 9 x x	♠ J x x	2 ♠	2 N-T
♥ x x	♥ x x	3 ♦	3 ♠
♦ A x x	♦ Q x x x	Pass	
♣ x	♣ Q x x x		

Responder (not vulnerable against vulnerable opponents) fears the worst when he hears opener announce less than a one-bid. Two no-trump is the safest psychic response.

Opener announces a maximum by bidding a new suit. Responder then confesses by going back to three spades, whereupon opener passes. If the opponents enter the auction now, they are one trick higher than if responder had passed.

Sequence 84

SOUTH	NORTH	SOUTH	WEST	NORTH	EAST
♠ A Q J x x x	♠ x x x x	2 ♠	Dble	3 ♥	Pass
♥ Q x x	♥ x x	3 ♠	Pass	Pass	?
♦ x x x	♦ A x x x				
♣ x	♣ x x x				

Responder's bid of three hearts is forcing, just as though the double had not taken place. This rather obvious psych will tend to confuse some opponents. At worst, it raises the level of bidding for the doubler's partner.

Sequence 85

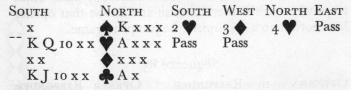

SOUTH	NORTH	SOUTH	WEST	NORTH	EAST
♠ x	♠ K x x x	2 ♥	3 ♦	4 ♥	Pass
♥ K Q 10 x x	♥ A x x x	Pass	Pass		
♦ x x	♦ x x x				
♣ K J 10 x x	♣ A x				

Responder expects opener to be short in diamonds and therefore thinks the hand is an excellent fit (as indeed it is). Over a pass, responder might have bid only three hearts.

Sequence 86

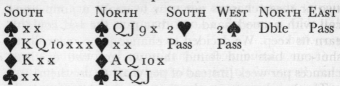

SOUTH	NORTH	SOUTH	WEST	NORTH	EAST
♠ x x	♠ Q J 9 x	2 ♥	2 ♠	Dble	Pass
♥ K Q 10 x x x	♥ x x	Pass	Pass		
♦ K x x	♦ A Q 10 x				
♣ x x	♣ K Q J				

A weak two-bid sometimes stirs the opponents up. In this case the penalty double should produce a two-trick or perhaps a three-trick set, yet opener has no game at hearts.

The double is made with the full knowledge that opener has a weak defensive hand. Hence responder should be sure of his ground and opener should be respectful of his partner's judgment.

Sequence 87

SOUTH	NORTH	SOUTH	WEST	NORTH	EAST
♠ x	♠ K 10 9 x	2 ♥	2 ♠	3 ♥	3 ♠
♥ K Q 10 x x x	♥ J x	Pass	4 ♠	Dble	Pass
♦ x x x	♦ A K x	Pass	Pass		
♣ K 10 x	♣ x x x x				

When the weak two-bid is used, many opponents suspect that they are being talked out of something—and sometimes they are. In this case, suspicion lands the opponents in a contract that should be set two or three tricks.

Jump Overcalls

At present most players have two ways to show a good hand when an opponent opens the bidding: they may make a jump overcall, or they may double for a take-out. This would be splendid except that it keeps a good healthy bid on a part-time job.

In the old days, my team-mates and I found perhaps two or three chances per year to make a jump over-call with a good hand. At that rate the bid couldn't earn its keep. We decided to change jump overcalls to shut-out bids and found that we got two or three chances per week (instead of per year) to use them.

That's why we made the change permanent. It wasn't that one bid was 'right' and another 'wrong'. It was simply that one bid was useful while the other was an expensive luxury.

For the same common-sense reason, we made an exception when vulnerable against non-vulnerable op-ponents. Perhaps once in a year you might want to bid a lot with a weak hand even under these unfavourable conditions. The rest of the year you would want to have solid strength for any jump bid with such vulner-ability.

To sum up, we use a jump overcall:

(a) as a pre-empt with equal vulnerability, or when not vulnerable against vulnerable opponents;

(b) to show a good hand when vulnerable against non-vulnerable opponents.

The player at your right deals and bids one spade. What do you bid with each of the hands that follow?

Neither side vulnerable

177. ♠ x x ♥ x ♦ Q J 10 x x x ♣ K Q J x

Bid three diamonds. This hand should win four dia-monds and at least two clubs, so it is unlikely to run into a disastrous penalty. The hand is far too weak for such a bid if you are vulnerable against non-vulnerable op-ponents. It is slightly too weak if both sides are vulnerable. You might bid three diamonds with slightly less if non-vulnerable against vulnerable opponents.

Opponents (only) vulnerable

178. ♠ Q x ♥ x x x ♦ A Q J 10 x x ♣ x x

Bid three diamonds. This hand may win only five tricks, but the honours will help protect you against severe loss. It would be unsound to bid three diamonds on so weak a hand under any other vulnerability conditions.

Both sides vulnerable

179. ♠ — ♥ x x ♦ A J 10 9 x x ♣ K J 10 x x

Bid three diamonds. This hand should produce close to seven tricks. (Nevertheless, it would be too weak for such a bid if you were vulnerable against non-vulnerable opponents.) Your partner raises with some such values as:

180. ♠ x x x ♥ K x x x x ♦ Q x x ♣ Q x

You have a play for four diamonds, if permitted to play there, while the enemy might well be able to make four spades. Even if you don't manage to steal the hand at four diamonds, you might profitably sacrifice at five diamonds. Normal bidding might shut out your partner instead of the opponents.

Your side (only) vulnerable

181. ♠ x x ♥ K x ♦ A K Q x x x x ♣ A x

Bid three diamonds. One test of such a jump to the level of three is that you should be willing to have your partner bid three no-trump with one sure stopper and about one fast trick on the side.

The player at your right deals and bids one heart. What do you bid with each of the following hands?

Neither side vulnerable

182. ♠ K J 10 x x x ♥ x ♦ Q J x x ♣ x x

Bid two spades. This hand should win at least five tricks at spades, yet it is not what you might call a 'good' hand.

Opponents (only) vulnerable

183. ♠ Q J 10 x x x ♥ x ♦ Q 10 x x ♣ x x

Bid two spades. This hand will probably win five tricks at spades but is next-to-worthless on defence. Curiously enough, you would not make an overcall of one spade with this garbage because your partner might think you had some slight defensive values. He will not count on you for any when you jump to two spades.

Both sides vulnerable

184. ♠ K Q 10 x x x ♥ x ♦ K Q 10 x ♣ x x

Bid two spades. You expect to win six tricks or more.

Your side (only) vulnerable

185. ♠ K Q 10 x x x ♥ x ♦ A K J x ♣ x x

Bid two spades. The playing strength is only slightly better than that of the last example, but there are fewer quick losers. The hand may well produce a game if partner can muster up a light raise.

Your side (only) vulnerable

186. ♠ A Q x x x x ♥ x ♦ K J x ♣ x x

Bid two spades. This hand is not nearly as good in top cards as the last example, but it is nearly as good for offence. You want to invite a light raise and therefore make the jump bid.

Partner's Action

When you have made a jump overcall, your partner knows what type of hand you have and can tell from his own hand:

(a) which side has most of the strength; and

(b) whether or not a sound suit is available for sacrifice or profit.

If the opponents have the strength, he can often raise you or make some bid that will confuse the enemy—provided he has some slight help for your suit. If he has a good hand, he may raise, double the enemy, or pass.

Sequence 88

WEST	EAST	The bidding (neither side
♠ A 10 9 x x x x	♠ Q x x	vul.):
♥ x	♥ x x x x	
♦ x x x	♦ x x	
♣ x x	♣ A J x x	

SOUTH	WEST	NORTH	EAST
1 ♥	2 ♠	Pass	3 ♠

East knows that West has a weak hand. Since his own hand also is weak, he fears that game can be made against him. His spade holding is good enough to continue West's pre-emptive tactics. Even if South is not silenced, his job has been made difficult.

Sequence 89

WEST	EAST	The bidding (E-W vul.):
♠ K Q J 10 x x x	♠ x x x	
♥ x	♥ x x x x	
♦ K Q	♦ x x	
♣ x x x	♣ A Q J x	

SOUTH	WEST	NORTH	EAST
1 ♥	2 ♠	Pass	3 ♠

This time East knows that West has a strong hand (because of the vulnerability). His raise is not designed to shut South out but to encourage West to proceed to game.

Sequence 90

WEST	EAST	The bidding (neither side
♠ Q J x x x x	♠ A x x x	vul.):
♥ x x	♥ x x x	SOUTH WEST NORTH EAST
♦ K 10 x x	♦ Q J x	1 ♥ 2 ♠ Pass 4 ♠
♣ x	♣ A Q x	

East knows that West has a weak hand, but knows that his own strength will surely fit any possible West hand. Curiously enough, there is a fair play for game at spades, while North-South may have an equally good play for game at hearts.

Sequence 91

WEST	EAST	The bidding (E-W vul.):
♠ A K Q J x x	♠ x x x	SOUTH WEST NORTH EAST
♥ x x	♥ x x x	1 ♥ 2 ♠ Pass 4 ♠
♦ K 10 x x	♦ A x x	
♣ x	♣ A x x x	

Compare with Sequence 90. East can afford a much lighter raise to game because West shows a far better hand with his overcall.

Sequence 92

WEST	EAST	The bidding (neither side vul.):
♠ K Q J 10 x x	♠ x x	SOUTH WEST NORTH EAST
♥ x x	♥ x	1 ♥ 2 ♠ Pass 3 ♦
♦ x x	♦ A Q J x x x	Pass 3 ♠ Pass 4 ♣
♣ x x x	♣ A K x x	Pass 4 ♠ Pass Pass
		Pass

East's bid of three diamonds is forcing on West for one round. East cannot bid three diamonds with a weak hand and no spade fit; he should pass and hope that the opponents fit just as badly.

When East bids a new suit at his second turn, he is clearly headed for game.

Sequence 93

West	East	The bidding (E.W vul.):			
♠ AQJ10xxx	♠ Kxxx	SOUTH	WEST	NORTH	EAST
♥ x	♥ xxxxx	1♥	2♠	Pass	3♦
♦ Kxx	♦ —	Pass	4♦	Pass	5♣
♣ Kx	♣ AQxx	Pass	5♦	Pass	5♠
		Pass	6♠	Pass	Pass
		Pass			

As in Sequence 92, East's bid of three diamonds is forcing; but this time to game. East can afford to cue-bid the diamonds and show club control before raising spades. West naturally proceeds to slam since it is evident that East had the spade raise up his sleeve all the time. If West were void of hearts he would cue-bid in that suit, and the partnership might reach a grand slam!

Pre-emptive Double Raises

The strong double raise is a very comfortable base for slam bidding when the opponents are too weak to bid. Once the opponents enter the auction, however, slam is usually out of the question. The double raise is then best used as a shut-out bid.

When an opponent has bid, imagine that he has made a take-out double, and raise accordingly. Your partner should rely on you for at least four trumps and about four playing tricks—but not for a good hand. As the examples show, you have other ways to bid a strong hand.

The bidding has proceeded:

SOUTH	WEST	NORTH	EAST
1♠	2♣	?	—

187.   ♠ Qxxx   ♥ xx   ♦ KQxxx   ♣ xx

Bid three spades. With luck, your hand will be worth

about four tricks. Your partner should either make three spades or be down only one even if he has a minimum opening bid.

188. ♠ Q J x x ♥ x ♦ K x x x x ♣ x x x

Bid three spades. This is slightly weaker in high cards than No. 187, but the distribution is better. There is also more reason to try a shut-out against a heart bid.

189. ♠ Q J x ♥ x ♦ K Q x x x ♣ x x x x

Bid two spades (not three spades). It is not safe to double raise with only three trumps. Your partner does not expect much strength of a double raise, but he has a right to expect four trumps.

190. ♠ Q J x x ♥ K x ♦ A Q J x x ♣ x x

Bid two diamonds. You expect to reach at least a game contract, but there is no need to make a jump bid. Your bid in a new suit is forcing for one round, and you can raise spades vigorously at your next turn.

The bidding has proceeded:

SOUTH	WEST	NORTH	EAST
1 ♥	1 ♠	Pass	?

191. ♠ K x x x ♥ J x ♦ J 10 x x x ♣ K x

Bid three spades. Where are all the high cards? Your partner could not double for a take-out, North had no free bid, and you have nothing to brag about. South must have a good hand, but your jump raise will make life difficult for him.

192. ♠ Q J x x ♥ x ♦ A K J x x ♣ A x x

Bid three diamonds. A jump bid in a new suit is forcing to game just as it would be if your partner had opened the bidding. A slam is not out of the question, even against a sound opening bid. With somewhat less strength you would bid four spades at once, or two diamonds. You would not, however, bid three spades with a strong hand.

Double Jump Responses

Opening pre-emptive bids of three or more contain a strong six-carder occasionally, but are usually based on a suit of at least seven cards. Strength is pretty much concentrated within the trump suit. The theory behind this usage is as follows:

1. A pre-emptive bid aptly describes the kind of hand and general amount of strength held by the bidder.

2. The best trump suit available to the partnership is most often the long suit bid.

3. Pre-emption makes difficult and risky for the enemy the finding of their best fit and especially the best *level* at which to play.

Many systems, many partnerships use such opening pre-emptives. Much less consideration has been given to the bidding of the same type of hand after the bidding has been opened.

When partner has opened with a bid of one of a suit, or has made a negative double of an opponent's bid of one of a suit, somewhat the same theory outlined above is effective, holding the same kind of hand.

Fortunately, there is available a bid, seldom used in most systems, for this purpose and pre-emptive effect. This is the double-jump response. To be most effective its range of high-card and playing strength should be narrow and well-defined.

The bidding has proceeded:

WEST	NORTH	EAST	SOUTH
1 ♦	Double	Pass	?

193. ♠ x x ♥ K J 10 x x x x ♦ x x x ♣ x

Bid three hearts. You describe a hand on which you might have opened with a pre-emptive bid. Your partner can count on you for five or six playing tricks if hearts are trumps. You deny holding as many as two aces or kings. You might have an ace or a king in a side suit but in that case your trump suit is queen high at best.

194. ♠ Q J x x x x ♥ x x ♦ x ♣ A 10 x

Bid three spades. Partner can pass with a shaded double or with an inappropriate hand. With a fit he should go on and if he should try for a slam you will gladly co-operate. Holding a side ace and generally a maximum for this response you will know that partner should find the quantity of your strength satisfactory, assuming that he understands the range of possible strength of a double jump response.

195. ♠ x ♥ Q J 10 x x x ♦ x x x ♣ K x x

Bid three hearts. If a one-heart bid is made you will have a difficult rebid problem. And then see how easy and safe it is for West to show a spade suit at the range of one. West can now find a fit at a profitable level or can find a lack of fit or strength and cautiously withdraw from the auction. Look at West's problem over three hearts. If he bids, North may have a double waiting. Or, North passing, there is a problem for East. He cannot know whether West has overbid under pressure or has the full value for the rebid. Finding their best suit and level will be much harder if the pre-empt is made.

196. ♠ A Q J x x x x ♥ x x ♦ x x ♣ Q x

Bid four spades. You have too much playing strength to stay out of game. This bid is better than a strength-showing two spade bid. Like its weaker brother the double jump response, the jump to game describes a hand of concentrated strength. Partner cannot take you to slam with two quick losers in any suit because you advise with this bid that you lack any top card in a side suit in addition to the ace of spades which he will also be lacking. If the opponents have a profitable sacrifice you are making it difficult to find. On the other hand they might be thus induced to take a phantom sacrifice. They will have to guess and decide what to do all in one bid.

The bidding has proceeded:

WEST	NORTH	EAST	SOUTH
1 ♦	Pass	?	—
or 1 ♥			

197.　♠ K Q 10 x x x x 　♥ x 　♦ J x 　♣ x x x

Bid three spades. Partner should rarely pass. Only with a spade singleton or void *and* a hand of minimum or shaded high-card strength is a pass in order. You solve your rebid problems with this clear description of your hand. You want to urge a spade game but cannot insist. In many possible auctions there will be no good later bids after first bidding one spade.

198.　♠ A J 10 x x x x 　♥ x x 　♦ x 　♣ K J x

Bid one (not three) spades. As the bidding develops your partner will know that you have side strength in addition to a good long spade suit. There might be advantages to pre-empting, but this is counter-balanced by the slams you will miss if you do pre-empt with such hands. It is most important to keep the range of strength narrow to aid the partnership in gaining the maximum from the bid.